CASTE AND CASTE CONFLICT IN RURAL SOCIETY

Caste and Caste Conflict in Rural Society

Ram Bali Mishra

Commonwealth

Caste and Caste Conflict in Rural Society

Edition : 2025

ISBN 81-7169-013-0

Published by :
Commonwealth Publishers (P) Ltd.
4831/24, Govind Lane,
Ansari Road, Darya Ganj,
New Delhi - 110002
Ph. : 23272541, 23242541
e-mail : commonwealthpublishers2016@gmail.com

Distributed by :
Arjun Publishing House
4831/24, Govind Lane,
Ansari Road, Darya Ganj,
New Delhi - 110002
Ph. : 23272541, 23242541
e-mail : arjunbooks2001@gmail.com

Printed at :
Milan Enterprises
Delhi

Preface

The present study is an outcome of the primary data, I have gathered in field situation during the years 1982-84. What motivated me to undertake the present problem was the conspicuous absence of the study of conflict in human behaviour by sociologists. The studies conducted in this area are very scant. A single psychological study on Pattern of Caste Tension is undertaken by Dr. K.K. Singh in Senapur village of Jaunpur district in U.P. in which Dr. Singh identifies the reasons why the Thakurs and Chamars of the village came at the stage of inter-caste tension.

It was for the first time that the German social scientist Karl Marx viewed class conflict in capitalistic system. Later on, Ralf Dahrendorf viewed the same phenomenon in industrial society. Although, modern era witnesses disruption in India's Hindu caste system, due to operation of numerous change factors responsible for creation of two opposite thrusts—one being upward from downward and other being downward from upward, but studies undertaken in this area are too scant and hence it deserved attention.

This study is divided into six chapters. Chapter I introduces the problem and its need for research. Chapter II mentions the geographical features, land acquired, main crops, and social amenities available in the studied villages. Chapter III deals with concepts used, techniques applied and variables taken. Chapter IV highlights the history of caste conflict starting from Vedic period till today. Chapter V aims at analysing the field data gathered from 200 respondents belonging to different castes while Chapter VI passes concluding remarks.

This empirical study is not a contribution on my part but the entire credit goes to my Hon'ble Supervisor Dr. B.D. Tripathi, Reader, Department of Sociology, Kashi Vidyapith. Varanasi who, in spite of his numerous academic as well as domestic problems, gave his most valuable time whenever I needed him. I express my gratitude to him. I am also obliged of my Principal Shri Pandit Ram Kumar Tripathi, B.N.K.B. Post-Graduate College, Akbarpur, Faizabad. I am grateful to my fellows Dr. Chandra Shekhar Mishra, Lecturer, Department of Sociology, Shri P.N. Mishra, Department of Psychology, Shri R.S. Mishra, Department of Education, B.N.K.B Post-Graduate College, Akbarpur, Faizabad who encouraged and inspired me. Ultimately, I thank Shri Rama Shankar Tripathi, Lecturer, Department of Sociology and Shri S.N. Gupta, Typist, Central Office, Kashi Vidyapith, Varanasi for their cordial support.

RAM BALI MISHRA

Contents

List of Tables

List of Illustrations

List of Photographs

1

Introduction

Cooperation and conflict are the fundamental ways of human interaction. Cooperation is evidenced when human beings work together for the realisation of common goals and values. When the goals and values are scarce so that they may not be shared compatibly, human beings strive against each other for their differential attainment. The resulting mode of inter-human behaviour is termed as conflict.[1] Social life is always characterized as an admixture of conflict and peace. In every society we observe the conditions of conflict inherent in every state of peace and likewise in every conflict the conditions of peace are prevalent. History witnesses that in all societies, may be contemporary or past, primitive or modern, we hardly find, even a single instance in which a society exists or has ever existed without social conflict in its system. At all ages and at all moments of time, there has been a simultaneous presence of agreements and disagreements, consensus and conflict present in almost all societies. All human relations are the relations of co-operation and conflict. Max Weber rightly points out that "conflict

1. P.N. Rastogi, 1975: *The Nature and Dynamics of Factional Conflict*, The Macmillan Company of India Ltd., Delhi, p. 1.

cannot be excluded from social life."[1] Therefore, this is a sociological occasion to pay greater attention to understand social conflict which is universal in nature.

Any knowledge or tendency to gain knowledge is assumed to emerge from within the social structure present. Society provides conditions necessary to think over it. That is why the structural imbalance or the state of disequilibrium produced or caused by social conflict in the French Society of the nineteenth century instigated and attracted Auguste Comte to tend to seek or search a Science crucial to explain and maintain the social order. Again, it was the same causation that made Professor Durkheim to identify a logical correlation between suicide rates and variation in social cohesiveness of the group.[2] The nineteenth century Europe keenly observed the total disruption and disintegration of feudal social system there. This has undermined all conflict-regulating mechanisms in the old social structure, social conflict emerged in great quantity and intensity, bringing about greater changes in almost all spheres of human activities in European countries. As a consequence, social conflict and the social changes brought by social conflict in old social structure of Europe became the focal point of imagination and discussion of many Sociologists and Social Scientists of this period. It is also important to note and notice that many Sociologists among whom Karl Marx, Emile Durkheim, Ward, Small and Veblen are main, became social reform-oriented due to revolutionary changes which took place in the nineteenth century Western Societies. Many of them were engaged in searching for the emergence of a new order and structure from the prevailing chaos (disorder) in the society. They thought conflict as "inherent in the social structure and those particular types of conflict which are accessed negatively could be uprooted, only

1. Max Weber: *The Methodolgy of Social Science*, (Trans.) E.A. Shils and N.A. Finch, The Free Press, Glencoe, Illinois, 1949, p. 26.
2. Emile Durkheim, *Suicide: A Study in Sociology*, Kegan Paul Ltd., London, 1966, pp. 297-360.

through structural change."[1] This period showed social conflict and social change as central theme for most of the sociological imaginations, works and writings. But this sociological curiosity, enthusiasm and orientation could remain no longer after thirties of this century.

The main reason for this shift in the focus for sociological studies can be investigated in the changes which have occurred in the Western societies since the beginning of this century. The high intensity social conflict which was strongly prevalent in the emerging capitalistic societies of the West in the nineteenth century gradually lowered down along with the structural changes. But these changes did not affect the basic values, statuses and roles, because the pattern of distributing scarce social values like power, prestige, wealth, rewards, etc., did not undergo much change and remained nearly as usual. Indeed, the groups which used to share and enjoy these scarce social values have been substituted; but the distribution pattern of structural elements remained more or less the same. The feudal overlords have been replaced by an emerging capitalistic group and the traditional roles of peasants have been assigned to the working class. These processes of group-substitutions in nineteenth century Western societies led to the convulsions, that is the contractions of muscles were observed in ninteenth century Western societies as an outcome of what we call the processes of group-substitutions or group-replacements. Eminent Scholar Max Weber has clearly analysed the existence and persistence of basic customs, traditions, values, statuses and roles throughout this period when the superstructure underwent change upto much extent at wider level in West.[2] After a bit duration, the modern industrial social structure of the West occupied a comparatively stable position somewhat similar to the kind of stability that existed and remained in the feudal social structure of the West before

1. Lewis A. Coser: *The Functions of Social Conflict*, Routledge and Kegan Paul Ltd., London, 1956, p. 19.

2. Max Weber: *The Protestant Ethic and Spirit of Capitalism* (Trans.) Talcott Parsons, Unwin University Books, London, 1968.

Industrial Revolution. Upto this period of time, when contemporary sociological thinkers had begun to emerge, the Western societies had attained a measure of structural stability. When the contemporary industrial societies emerged, structural stability rather than instability became the major point of attraction of Western thinkers. When the focus of attention of sociologists of this period shifted from dynamic aspect of social structure of West to its static aspect, it is not wonderful that contemporary sociological research "concentrated more on the technique ways of social investigation and somewhat less on the discovery and formulation of broad substantive theories concerning basic formulation of socio-cultural problems."[1] Now, social conflict is no more studied as an important agent responsible to bring about structural changes. On the other hand, many contemporary Western functionalists like Parsons sees conflict as "deviance" and prescribes and describes it in a socio-psychological fashion.[2] The efforts made by Elton Mayo to present the explanation of labour strikes in terms of deviant or disorganized personalities of trade union leaders are the best suitable and classic examples of the extent to which functionalism has gone. Thus, it will not be an over-statement if we infer that sociologists in recent periods have been satisfied to leave the scientific study of conflict where Simmel left it.[3]

In this way, it seems that Indian Sociology and Western both are in no respect dissimilar to each other in approaches. In what respect does predominant Western-oriented Indian Sociology vary from its Western counterpart is only on the ground that it focusses on two societies which are widely dissimilar in structure and development. Although contemporary Indian society has undergone a greater change and has become structurally quite disintegrated due to numerous of factors operating on Indian scene, they are yet desirable to be given

1. P.A. Sorokin: *Sociological Theories of Today*, Harpar and Row, New York, 1966, p. 6.
2. Talcott Parsons: *The Social System*, The Free Press, Glencoe, Illinois, 1951, pp. 280-281.
3. Lewis A. Coser, op. cit., p. 17.

sociological treatments. The Indian Sociologists must be concerned in dealing with such structural disintegration and change which are essential features of contemporary India. But there is nothing strange in the fact that the Indian Sociologists have not done any significant work towards an understanding of the changes which are taking place in Indian Society.

As far as Indian Sociology is concerned, it can afford to relegate studies on social conflict and social change to secondary importance. Post-Independence India has witnessed a wide occurrence of social tensions and conflicts. This happened soon after independence when national government introduced several new legislations, legal reforms to recognize the Panchayats, abolish Zamindari and to outlaw untouchability. These legislative measures have rudely shaken the very foundation of the traditional pattern of social interaction in the community consisting of different castes living for generations under fairly amicable conditions. The conflict-regulating mechanisms like the practice of keeping social distance between different castes and the hereditary allocation of occupational roles which controlled drastic structural changes have been abolished all of sudden. In the Hindu community, the different castes have now begun to view each other with suspicion, hate and fear. The concept and provision of equality have been extended to all spheres of social life without corresponding changes in other respects, thereby bringing about a complete breakdown of institutionalized conflict-regulating arrangements. What we have to bear in mind is that most of these changes are from without[1] and not from within as was the case in Western societies, and these changes in their turn made many of the dynamically variable elements within the structure to affect further drastic changes in the structure of which these elements are a part. When such changes bring about structural imbalances, which in their turn led to further changes in the structure, we cannot attribute them to certain "strains" in the integrated systems. There-

1. Talcott Parsons, op. cit., p. 487.

fore, the sociological studies relating to Indian society should have more bearing on conflict and change rather than on integration and stability.

Hindu India is a caste-ridden and caste-structured society. Here every individual is certainly a member of a particular caste. Every caste is an endogamous social group having a definite set of rules called council to control over its members who are ascribed a permanent social status on the basis of birth, having a common traditional occupation, a particular name and whose members bear a particular life style. The whole Hindu society is characterized by a system universally known as caste system. This caste system is nothing but hierarchically arranged endogamous social groups called castes in which all the constituent units or groups are attributed a traditional occupation. The system has, since antiquity, certain rules, and norms, regarding social intercourse, marriage, food taking, etc. Hindu caste system prescribes a definite standard of social behaviour for all castes in varying degrees. This social prescription for every caste unit to behave in different manners has naturally given rise to what we call social cleavages among different castes. Besides these, there are also other socio-economic conditions prevailing in Indian society that have led to tension and conflict in rural Indian caste system. An elaboration of these conditions can be clearly cited here.[1] Power which in India has always flowed from above downwards now flows from below upwards. The administration of the village was indeed always, even in Muslim and British times, mainly by the people of the village. But the village was concerned only with the small issues of its own narrow surroundings. Now, for the first time, it is the villager's vote which decides how the die shall be cast in larger national issues also. One of the world's oldest, most unchanging, and most devout peasant societies is adjusting itself to the new industrial world the last hundred years have created. The change which is taking place in rural India is a change none-the-less revolutionary for being comparatively peaceful.

1. The Pionneer, 1984, Wednesday, January 25, p. 6.

The economic revolution in rural India is only beginning. It is not, however, enough for India to need an economic transformation and for the electorate to vote for it. There must also be a change in the public's standard of values to make it possible institutions like castes are impracticable in an industrial society. The great Indian question mark is, therefore, whether they will change quickly enough for a revolution to be averted. No society in the world today is changing more quickly than the India.

Perhaps the most convincing evidence that the system is in a state of crisis is the outbreak in a more pronounced form than ever before of conflict between castes themselves, now often a little more than the traditional shell enclosing the kernel of modern economic and class interests. It is not a coincidence that this conflict is taking its most virulent form in those states where the Janata Party was in power for about three years. In these states, notably Uttar Pradesh, the most populous in the country, Bihar, the least developed, and Madhya Pradesh, the largest in terms of area—the emergence of Janata Party marked the ascendance of officially listed backward castes whose pre-Janata Party organs were parties like Jana Sangha, and the Bhartiya Lok Dal.

Some of them like Jats and Yadavas and Kurmis in Uttar Pradesh, and Kurmis, Koeris and Yadavas in Bihar have become quite prosperous over the past thirty years partly because of the effeteness of the traditional upper castes and partly because, like the European bourgeoisies in relation to feudal classes, of their dynamism, thrift and hard work assisted by the ability to corner investments in development. With economic success has come confidence, aggressiveness and political ambition. Having once shored up the upper castes, they now want to take up their place. Their prosperity, however, depends, in turn, on keeping landless agricultural labour in the countryside and the unemployed proletariat in the urban centres, in both cases often from the Harijan castes, where they are—at the bottom of the heap. But, these caste groups, too, have expectations of social mobility and economic gain, are becoming aware of the real value of their so far prodigally given labour and learning to organise and fight for their rights.

Evidently, the so-called backward group and Harijans are on a collision course, whereas in Uttar Pradesh, Bihar, Madhya Pradesh, and Karnataka, the ascendant backward castes seek to institutionalise their gains by, for instance, reserving 26 per cent of government jobs for their own kinsmen—this was widely misconstrued as an attempt by the Janata Party to widen its social base when, in fact, it was an effort to consolidate its existing social base—the result is prolonged and violent.

One feature of the caste/class war being waged throughout the country at present deserves notice. The Janata Party—more precisely now, the Bhartiya Janata Party, the Lok Dal—represents essentially, a different coalition of caste/class interests than the Congress did for some three decades. Since the aggressive rural backward castes in league with the urban trading/petty shopkeepers came to power for three years, a caste/class war started and is so much in evidence today. Since the Harijans are immediately in collusion with the backward castes the battle between the two will occupy the centre of the stage for some time to come. The battle with the Congress (I), ostentatiously on the side of the Harijans, is now well and truly joined.

The other notable aspects of the caste war, and especially that between the Harijans and the upper castes, is that it is taking place mainly, though not, exclusively, in the villages and small towns. Significantly cities are relatively free of such clashes. The conflict in the cities is generally subtle, covert. It operates within a different framework and has a different set of rules. The imperatives of urbanization have promoted social co-existence, if not integration. Atomisation, anonymity, the myriad pressures of time and work, the number of roles each individual is compelled to play in his interaction with a wide range of social groups, the jostling juxtaposition of disparate cultures, such attributes of modernity combine to make social life quite different from that in the countryside. Caste is a factor in this bewildering plurality, but, unlike in village and small towns, it is not the overwhelming one. No wonder the Harijans prefer to live and work in major, especially public, industries in cities and large towns where caste does not matter quite so much and it is easier to escape the harsh social effects of one's low birth and poverty.

Paradoxically, the caste war is much more and much more blatantly in evidence in the countryside because villages and small towns are becoming less and less like they have always been. Modernity, no matter how superficial a form, is penetrating them and the traditional order is under attack. What US Sociologists like to call social change as occurring much faster than is possible under the traditional set-up in those regions where such penetration is considerable.

Some facts regarding intercaste tension reflect in the scholarly work undertaken by Chitambar.[1] He has tried to draw rural sociological scene of inter-relation between higher and lower castes. He sees the existing caste system in rural society as disrupted due to technological advancement, process of mechanization in agricultural sector of rural population industrialization and modern communication. Due to these factors, where on one hand, Chitambar observes the disruption of the system, on the other hand, he observes the increasing conflict in traditional roles. Caste occupation and consequent roles are replaced by remunerative occupations, perhaps in nearby factories.[2] "Social stratification may "set the stage for interstratum rivalry and conflict. Such conflict may take various forms but in general results from an upthrust from lower strata to share equal rights with the upper strata and down thrust from upper strata to keep lower strata in their

1. J.B. Chitambar: *Introductory Rural Sociology*, John Wiley and Sons, New York, 1973, p. 83.
2. Ibid., p. 83.

place. Such conflict frequently occurs when stratification systems are weakening, or in the process of disintegration being subjected to a variety of influential forces within society such as new ideologies, pressure groups, collective frustration of lower strata, and/or political and other interest groups. Examples of this phenomenon in operation are in the caste system in India, and in racial conflicts in the U.S.A., South Africa, and countries newly independent or immediately prior to achievement of independence from colonialism."[1]

If social life is the admixture of peace and conflict, the ratio of peace and conflict in this amalgam is always in varying proportion. Sometimes, the amount or intensity and gravity of peace becomes greater, and sometimes, conflict shows its greater intension. The latter is more obvious and more true in modern era. Our entire social life is surrounded by tension and conflict today. If a dictionary of conflict is aimed to be built up and if this task is undertaken by an expert, a vast body of millions of words regarding this phenomenon would be an outcome of this painstaking greater task. Not only our kitchens but the whole globe is eclipsed by this reality. The entire cosmos is interwoven by the fabrics of conflict. Our social relations have become interest-based. All the communities on the earth are passing through a great crisis. "We feeling" is loosening and is being replaced by strong hold of "they feeling." Communities are being substituted by associations. Our relations are becoming ad-hoc. A process of "satisfy need and run-away" is operating at larger scale in almost all walks of human life. "Our entire social structure has become unsystemic, disintegrated. Whole social environment has become polluted. Modern age is the age of anomie. Large scale deviance in all sectors of human life is displaying a naked dance. The Indian jointness, its collectivity, its

1. Ibid., p. 233.

community and Indian nationalism, they all are shivering."[1]

Indian society is characterized by caste. For some, Indian society is equal to caste. This question is true in the sense that caste is the pivot of Indian society or it is the fundamental element of Indian nation. If this fact is overlooked or if this central or soul-element is taken out of the Indian social domain, perhaps Indian society shall not be able to maintain its identity as it has maintained so far, and if any scholar wants to know such India which has eradicated its 'caste' element, he shall have to march in the way to search out a new definition of casteless India. But, what shall be the structure of such casteless Indian society, it cannot be explored at this stage. Whether it shall look like class-based open society as occident looks or something else, it is just a question mark and is not so easy to be answered at this moment. It is, obviously, very difficult and shall be very difficult to understand such a new phenomenon. The relationship between Indian society and its caste system is analogous to the relationship between body and soul. The human body is useful only when it has a soul. In absence of a soul, it is dead, it is useless, it is rather something else other than living body. Like this, Indian society without its caste system shall be other than this one. Now, what shall be the difference between caste based Indian society and casteless Indian society?, it is just a matter of sociological invention with a high level of abstraction. Naturally, both shall differ from each other in numerous of aspects. If this argument is true, caste is one of the most important institution directly responsible to strengthen 'National solidarity' and integration. Any sort of disruption in caste system shall cause disruption in national unity.

National disintegration, today, has become a central theme of public discussion. Not only the intellects but even commoners make it as the issue of their talks and speeches.

1. R.B. Mishra: The Paper submitted for Seminar on 'New Education' organised by Avadh University, Faizabad at Butlar Palace, Lucknow, U.P., Feb. 11-12, 1984.

For politicians meant for opposition, it is a burning matter and material, it is a device to propagate the government's inefficiency, to blame and defame its social image and ultimately to pull its leg behind. It is also a tool for leaders in opposition to create a negative attitude in the public towards ruling government and to frame a public opinion negative for the government but conducive for their chances in further election.

Caste disintegration is the root cause of so-called national disintegration. Indian caste system of today has been twisted out of shape. Every caste unit has segregated from other caste units. The members of each and every caste are confined only to their own caste. This phenomenon or behaviour is caste-patriotism attributed to the members of a caste. Caste considerations are playing a significant role in all human activities. Thus, Indian society has become a casteocratic society. Although, this casteocratic attitude is latent and inherent in Indian minds, but considaring some or sometimes all the criteria as universalistic, caste criterion is given due weightage which is an important feature of developing society. If one has to search a social order, he shall have to trace out the drawbacks of Indian caste system. It is with this view in mind that the present study has been undertaken.

Although, there are four Tehsils in Faizabad district, but for the present study only one Tehsil of this district has been chosen. This is known as Akbarpur Tehsil. Other Tehsils are Faizabad, Bikapur and Tanda. The acute form of casteism, caste prejudices, caste tension and conflict is more prevalent in the villages of Akbarpur, therefore, its villages as setting have been given due consideration. Again, the more acute form of caste tension and conflict in villages of Akbarpur block is manifest, therefore, researcher is confined for this study to the villages of Akbarpur block. In this region, at Tehsil level, there is forward-backward caste conflict, though most of the villages are victim of intra-backward, intra-forward, intra-scheduled caste, scheduled caste backward, scheduled caste forward and forward-backward caste conflicts. These are broadly the six models which any sociologist can take into account to deal with. Some of these models (three) have been identified by the researcher in neighbouring villages lying in the radius of ten kilometres from Akbarpur town. They are forward-backward, backward-backward and backward scheduled caste conflict, and they have been chosen for sociological analysis. Other rest models have been deliberately omitted due to research limitation and the limitation of researcher.

2

The Universe of Study

Faizabad is one of the eastern district of Uttar Pradesh and occupies a central position in the division of the same name. It lies between Lat. 26° 9′ and 26° 50′ N. and Long. 81° 40′ and 83° 8′ E. and in shape is a fairly regular parallelogram with a projection on the north-east jutting into the district of Azamgarh. The greatest length of the district from west to east is 90 miles and the greatest width from north to south 28 miles. Since the adjustment of 1869, when the area of the district was reduced from 2,344 to 1,689 square miles, there have been no major alterations in the boundaries of the district except those that occurred due to the changes in the course of the Ghaghra. Thus in 1899 (at the end of the second settlement) the area of the district increased to about 1,726 square miles (going up to 1739.6 square miles in 1904) and then decreased again to 1714 square miles in 1941 when the third Settlement was completed. At the time of the census of 1951 the area of the district was only 1,710 square miles. According to the census of 1971, the total geographical area of the district is 4,427 square kilometres. The district Faizabad consists of four Tahsils namely Tahsil Faizabad Sadar,

Sources: 1. District Gazetteer, Fyzabad, 1928.
2. Uttar Pradesh District Gazetteers, Faizabad, 1960.

Bikapur, Akbarpur and Tanda Tahsil. For the purpose of present study, the Tahsil Akbarpur has been selected. Specifically, some villages of Akbarpur block where the caste conflict has been acutely observed, have been purposively taken into account. It is contextual, therefore, to mention some of the essential features of Akbarpur pertaining to its socio-economic, cultural and geographical aspects.

The capital of the Tahsil Akbarpur is a considerable town lying in latitude 26°26′ north and longitude 80°32′ east, at a distance of 36 miles by road from Faizabad and 12 miles from Tanda. It lies on the Luchnow-Mughalsarai (Faizabad loop) line of the Northern Railway. The Government Roadways ply a bus between Faizabad town and Akbarpur, the road being a metalled one. Other bus routes run to Azamgarh and Tanda. Akbarpur is built on the left bank of the Tons. After the floods of 1955, a new Cement Concrete Bridge, which is an extension of the old one, has been built on the river. Metalled and unmetalled roads connect the town to Faizabad, Jaunpur, Tanda, Iltifatganj, Ramnagar, Kichhauchha and Shahzadpur. North-West from the town a road goes to Amsin and Gauhaniya. Roads also run from this place to Jalalpur, Maharua and Dostpur in the Sultanpur district.

Akbarpur was founded in the days of Akbar by Muhammad Mohsin who was incharge of the old pargana of Sinjhauli. He built a fort, high on the left bank of the Tons. It is said that in former days the place was covered with jungle and that Saiyed Kamal, a holy man, residing there was killed by robbers and buried within the precincts of the fort in which his tomb is still to be seen. Muhammad Mohsin Khan also built a mosque and the bridge over the Tons. The former stands in the fort where the Tahsil buildings are now located. It bears an inscription in Persian stating that this officer constructed it in the reign of Akbar when Munim Khan Khan-i-Khanan was the Governor of Avadh in 976 Hijri. The bridge in its original form was entirely of masonry and beyond it on the right is a large embarkment parly of masonry which extends eastward for some distance. Later some of the piers were removed and the arches replaced by girders. The great strength and solidity of the structure may be judged from the age and condition of the surviving original portions. On the north face is a stone slab with a Persian inscription bearing the name of the builder and the date which is the same as the date given in the inscription in the mosque. These buildings are said to have been erected in compliance with the directions of the Emperor himself, given when he passed through the place was a mint-town from Jaunpur to Agra. The place was a mint-town under the name of Akbarpur-Tanda. Shahjahanpur and Shahzadpur, on the opposite bank of the river, are named after the emperor's grandson of Shahjahan. Since that time Akbarpur has been the capital of the pargana of the same name and its history is chiefly connected with that of the Saiyed house of Pirpur. There is a large imambara and a number of mosques, the finest being situated in Shahjahanpur across the river.

Besides the tahsil headquarters, Akbarpur has a police station, the munsif's court. It has a hospital, a maternity centre and a velerinary hospital. A Post and Telegraph Office as well as a telephone public call office also exist in Akbarpur. There are three Intermediate Colleges, two for boys and one for girls. One Post-graduate College with Post-graduation in three Subjects viz., Sociology, Economics and Hindi with the provision of co-education is also there. There are some Junior High Schools and Primary Schools also for imparting education to boys and girls.

The Tahsil Akbarpur forms the south-eastern sub-division of the district Faizabad extending from the Pachhimrath pargana of Bikapur on the west to the boundary of Azamgarh district on the east. To the north lie pargana Amsin of Tahsil Faizabad and parganas Birhar and Tanda of the Tanda Tahsil, and to the south are the Baraunsa and Aldeman pargana of Sultanpur and vargana Mahul of Azamgarh, from all of which the Tahsil is separated by the Majholi rizer. Akbarpur is made up of four parganas, Majhaura in the west, Akbarpur in the middle and Surhurpur in the middle and Surhurpur in the East and Mahrua in South. The pargana Surhurpur was formerly included in Tanda Tahsil, but has now been included in Akbarpur Tahsil, since 1904. Akbarpur Tahsil is the biggest Tahsil according to area and population. According to 1971 Census report, the geographical area of Akbarpur Tahsil is 592241 with a population density of 426 persons per square kilometre and there are 905v illages. But the Census report 1981 shows that the total population of this tahsil is 727963, out of which 373133 are males and 354830 females. The population growth of this area during 1971-1981 is 135722 and therefore, population growth per annum is given by 13572.2 persons per annum. The Scheduled Caste populatipn of this Tahsil is 173871 out of which males are 89105 and females are 84768.

The total number of literates in Akbarpur Tahsil is 176913 out of which 135964 indicates male literacy while 40949 indicates female literacy. The number of illiterate males is 237169 and that of female illiterates is 313881. These figures calculated in terms of percentage literacy/illiteracy can be shown as under.

Table 2.1

Sl.No.	*Sex*	*Literacy* (%)	*Illiteracy* (%)
1.	Male	18.67	32.57
2.	Female	5.62	43.11

Source : Census Report (Manuscript), 1981.

The data show that the ratio of literacy between males and females is nearly 3 : 1 and the ratio of male-female illiteracy is 3 : 4. It is drained by several rivers: the Majholi flows along the southern border, the Marha enters the tahsil at the north-west corner of Mijhaura and the Biswi meanders through the middle of the western flank of the tahsil. After traversing Mijhaura, the Marha and the Biswi join each other on the western boundary of Akbarpur pargana and the combined stream, known as the Tons, flows through this pargana and that of Surhapur. It is navigable by boats of fair size as far as Jalalpur in the dry season and as far as Akbarpur in the rains. The little river Tirwa forms the northern boundary of the Tahsil for a short distance and further east the Tonri flows along the borders of Surjurpur and Birhar. Topographical variations are chiefly due to swamps, usar (bareen) and jungle patches and natural differences in the soil. There is fertile loam, sandy in places, in the well-drained tracts in the centre of Mijhaura, in the north of pargana Akbarpur and in the south of pargana Surhurpur. The greater part of pargana Akbarpur south of the Tons is a sea of usar containing scattered islands of cultivation. Elsewhere the stretches of usar are broken up by shallow lakes and patches of dhak jungle now being cleared so that more and more land is being brought under the plough. Generally early rice is the staple crop, its success depending upon regular and well distributed rainfall. Drainage is defective in the swampy area bordering the Tirwa and the Tonri rivers but the floods, when they come, are not serious. Numerous Jheels overflow in a wet year but any possible damage is more than offset by their usefulness as a scurce of cheap and easy irrigation. The other souces of irrigation are tanks, wells, canals and tubewells.

The Tahsil is well provided with means of communications. It has the benefit of the Lucknow-Mughalsarai (Faizabad loop) line of the Northern Railway which traverses it diagonally from Gosainganj, just outside the western corner, to Malipur in the south-east. Parallel to this line runs a first class metalled provincial highway from Faizabad to Jaunpur, with an avenue of trees. There are metalled roads leading from Akbarpur to Tanda and from Malipur railway station to Jalalpur. Of the metalled roads passing through Akbarpur Tahsil the most important are those from Tanda to Jaunpur. From Akbarpur to Maharua, from Akbarpur to Sultanpur and those leading from Jalalpur to Baskhari, Chahora and Tighara.

The most important bridges in the Tahsil are in Akbarpur and in Surhurpur, the former being on the Tons and the latter on the Majholi. There is also a girder bridge on the Tirwa at Ukara on the road from Akbarpur to Iltifatganj. Temporary bridges are constructed only during the cold weather on the roads crossing the Marha and the Biswi and on the Tons at Jalalpur. A bridge has been built on the Marha near Gosainganj on the road to Bhiti. There are public ferries at Jalalpur, Basohri and Mijhaura. Besides these there are several private ferries which ply across the Tons and the other rivers.

The headquarters of the Development Blocks of Bhiti, Katehri, Akbarpur, Jalalpur and Bhiaon are located within the Tahsil.

Most of the villages of Akbarpur Tahsil are smaller in size having population less than 500. These villages number 477. There are 241 middle sized villages having population of 500-1000. The number of big villages are 143 and rest are biggest villages with a population more than 2000. These data show that 52.7% of the villages of Akbarpur Tahsil are small villages.

Akbarpur Tahsil is well equipped by irrigational facilities for harvesting. The number of canals is 24. The size of canal per square kilometre is 86.0. There are 157 government tube-wells. The number of private tube-wells is 5386. Ponds, Jhils, etc. figure 2116 and the pakka wells number 4951. A precisely greater number of irrigational facilities available for the people of this area indicates that the farmers of Akbarpur rural area have not to depend now on the mercy of

Table 2.2

Block-wise Irrigational Facilities

Block	*No. of Canals*	*Canals per Sq. Km.*	*Govt. Tube Wells*	*Private Tube Wells*	*Pond, Jhil etc.*	*Pakka Wells*	*Percentage*
Akbarpur	11	47.0	41	1597	316	1614	28.33
Bhiti	1	1.0	43	890	586	156	13.27
Bhiaon	—	—	20	415	239	919	12.60
Jalalpur	—	—	20	1034	388	1439	22.80
Katehri	12	38.0	33	1450	587	823	23.0
Total	24	86.0	157	5386	2116	4951	100.0

Source: "Report of Executive Engineer (Canal)", Faizabad (1977-78).

clouds. They have now realized a sense of security for their cultivation, have made them quite prosperous to enhance their socio-economic and political status.

The table shown above reveals that the larger percentage of irrigational facilities (28.83%) are attributed to the villages of Akbarpur. The greatest span of canal's network spread over the fields of Akbarpur rural area (47.0 canals per square kilometre) provides the opportunity for the people of this area to think over the irrigation problem as an easiest task. Then comes Katehri block with 38.0 canals per square kilometre. In the jurisdiction of this block the percentage of irrigational facilities is 23. Jalalpur is ranked on third place while Bhiti and Bhiaon blocks have got nearly equal percentage of irrigational provisions.

So far as the distribution of agricultural tools and instruments is concerned, they are mentioned like this: the number of inland ploughs is 1052. Cultivators are 80, winnowing fans number 40; power threshers are 132, and other machines useful for agricultural instruments are 2800. Out of these 2800 agricultural instruments, 546 (19.50%) instruments are distributed in villages of Bhiti block; 443 (15.82%) agricultural instruments are spread in rural area of Bhiaon block; 543 (19.39%) instruments are in villages of Jalalpur block, the villages of Akbarpur block have been distributed 882 (29.32%) agricultural instruments and the rural people of Katehri block have got the advantage of 447 (15.96%) agricultural tools and devices. From these data regarding distribution of agricultural instruments, it is obvious that the people of Akbarpur block have got good deal of occasion to use greater number of agricultural devices. Next comes Bhiti block and least number of such devices characterize Bhiaon block.

Source : Sankhyikiya Patrika, District Faizabad, 1978.

Rice, wheat and maize are the main crops of Akbarpur Tahsil. These crops yield more output. The former two crops are the economic pivot of the people of this tahsil. These crops have beeen surveyed by Bhu Lekh Adhikari during the year 1977-78. Blockwise table is presented on page 23.

The data given in this table show that during 1977-78, wheat was the main crop in Akbarpur block, other crops (say) rice and maize were found absent. However, rice and maize do not remain uncropped generally.

The rural people of Akbarpur Tahsil who are engaged in works other than cultivation have been classified in numerous occupational and professional categories. According to 1961 Census, in all there are 20,239 persons who are engaged in economic activities other than cultivation. Out of these persons, 14,329 are males and 5,910 females. The ratio of either sex engaged in non-cultivating profession is approximately 5:2. A greater portion of these occupants (57.98%) is busy in craftsmanship, production process works etc.; 4.90% rural people are professional and technical workers; 2.7% persons are administrative, executive and managerial workers; 2.60% persons are engaged in other related jobs; 11.23% persons are sales workers; 8.45% persons are farmers, fishermen, hunters, laggers and other like works; 0.14% that is a very less number (3 persons) of persons are miners, quarrymen and related workers; 1.58% persons work in transport and communication departments; 8.38% workers work in sport and recreational activities; 2.13% workers are those who have not been classified by occupation.

For the purpose of present study, four villages from Akbarpur block have been selected. These are Ashrafpatti Newada, Panjupur (Newada), Rabipur Bhauddinpur (Bahauddinpur) and Hazipur Marui. There is inter-village

Source : Report of Bhu Lekha Adhikari, Faizabad, 1977-78.

Table 2.3

The Crops giving more Yield in Akbarpur Tahsil

Block	*Rice*		*Wheat*		*Maize*	
	Total Area (Hect.)	*Irrigated Area (Hect.)*	*Total Area (Hect.)*	*Irrigated Area (Hect.)*	*Total Area (Hect.)*	*Irrigated Area (Hect.)*
Bhiti	1295	–	1524	1510	1	–
Bhiaon	1583	–	440	440	–	–
Jalalpur	1390	70	781	780	2	–
Akbarpur	–	–	1291	1289	–	–
Katehri	4114	40	1437	1430	1	–
Total	8382	110	5473	5449	4	–

forward-backward caste conflict between Ashrafpatti Newada and Panjupur (Newada); intra-village backward-backward caste conflict in Rabipur Bhauddinpur (Bahauddinpur) village; and intra-village backward-scheduled caste conflict in Hajipur Marui village.

The Village Ashrafpatti Newada

The village is situated at the distance of 11 Kms. from Akbarpur town on Akbarpur-Baskhari pakka road. The village acquires an area of 64 acres. There have been 35 occupied residential houses and 35 households, according to 1971 Census report as mentioned in district handbook of Faizabad, series 21 and B, with a total population of 176 out of which 95 are males and 81 are females but manuscript of Census report 1981 reveals that this total number has increased to 211 out of which males are 104 and females are 107. The number of households has now increased from 35 to 43. The Scheduled Castes figure 27 out of which 16 are males and 11 are females. The picture of literacy including education is like that: male population figures 30 while female population figures 4 only. This indicates that in this village only 16.11% of the total population is literate and educated. This also indicates that most of the villagers are illiterates. Male population shows higher literacy (14.81%) in comparison to female population (1.9%). The number of illiterate males is 74 (35%) and that of illiterate females is 103 (48.81%). This shows that nearly three-fourth of the total village population is illiterate. The number of persons who worked at any time during last year is 121 out of which 58 are male and 63 are female workers. The number of female workers is greater than that of the male workers.

There is no provision of educational institution nor medical facilities like primary health centres and hospitals in the village. However, the people of this village for such ameni-

Source : 1. Census Report, 1961.
2. Census Report, 1971.

ties depend upon school situated at Kurki Bazar nearly two miles away from the village towards Akbarpur town. Private medical practitioners are the only medical alternatives for the people. There is no provision of electric supply in the village and the whole village remains unelectrified. The village is equipped by wells and hand-pipes for drinking water. The wheat and barley are cultivated by the people of the village as staple food.

Caste Distribution

The village consists of four castes. These are Brahmins, Kahar, Bhar and Chamar. Caste-wise distribution of households is given in Table 2.4.

Table 2.4

S. No.	*Castes*	*No. of Households*	*Percentage*
1.	Brahmin	2	4.65
2.	Kahar	1	2.32
3.	Bhar (Rajbhar)	33	76.74
4.	Chamar	7	16.27
	Total	43	100.00

This table shows that 76.74% of the total households belong to Bhar caste. This also indicates that Bhar caste is in majority. Other castes like Brahmin (4.65%), Kahar (2.32%) and Chamar (16.27%) are in minority. The Bhar caste being in majority dominates the village scene in many ways like social, economic, political and cultural. Most of the Bhar caste population cultivate their lands and are also farm labourers. These Bhars constitute 87.5% of the total Bhar caste population. The village is located by brick-kiln industry and this industrial pursuit has opened a new avenue for these people to select the alternative job and change their traditional occupation. 6.06% of Bhar households have not their own grain shops and have occupationally become traders. One member of Bhar caste named Ram Nath works in Telephone department at Delhi. One member Baij Nath is compounder of a private medical practitioner and another member known as Budhi Ram is gardener. The occupational class categorisation of heads of Bhar caste is presented in Table 2.5.

Table 2.5

S. No.	*No. of Persons in Bhar Caste*	*Occupations*
1.	28	Own land cultivation plus working as labourer in brick-kiln-industry.
2.	2	Grain shop keeping plus own land cultivation plus working as labourer in brick-kiln-industry.
3.	1	Working in Telephone at Delhi.
4.	1	Compounder plus own land cultivation plus working as labourer in brick-kiln-industry.
5.	1	Gardener.
Total	33	

Out of two Brahmin families, one is landless and another has 5 bighas of land. The landlord Brahmin family members cultivate own land and one of its members is in service.

Chamars of the village have got very less landlord which they cultivate themselves and also they are engaged as agricultural labourers.

There is only one family of Kahar which serves the village people on different occasions when it is called on.

The opening of brick-kiln industries in rural areas, industrialization at urban centres and towns and urbanization have opened the various avenues for working rural population to shift from traditional occupation to modern occupation. Also, the farm workers have begun to depart from farm working to other working places as they were paid a very low wage by landlord high castes, which was insufficient for their livelihood. The temptation and even payment of higher wages to the worker in non-agricultural concern have resulted in break-up of landlord higher caste and farm worker lower caste social relations. Not only this but even farm worker lower caste persons threat the higher caste-landlord not to plough their fields if the latter pay low wage or behave badly with the former. The threat by lower caste working rural population to the higher caste landlords not to plough their fields is common in rural areas today. Whenever tension takes place between these two social groups in villages, the higher caste persons are immediately threatened by lower caste persons of non-occupation. Today, the lower caste working persons think their services to higher caste landlords as a cooperation and obligation to them. They ignore them with the plea that they get wage in turn of their services.

Panjupur (Newada)

This is a hamlet of Panjupur village council called purwa. This hamlet is situated at the distance of 11 kms on Akbarpur-Baskhari pakka road. This hamlet is just on north side of the village Ashraf Patti Newada. Geographically, Panjupur Newada and Ashrafpatti Newada seem to be a single village but on paper both belong to different village councils. There is no fixed boundary line between the two, however, a Kachcha wall of nearly 7 feet height separates the two. The hamlet occupies a total area of 125 acres out of which 120 acres are cultivated. There are 30 households with a population of 200. The total number of literates are 120 out of which 90 are males and 30 are females. The ratio of male-female literacy is 3:1. In this hamlet, there is no scheduled caste and scheduled tribe. The hamlet does not have any educational institution of any standard. The boys and girls have to go to seek admission in an educational institution upto High School standard situated on pakka road at Kurki Bazar nearly two miles away from the hamlet towards Akbarpur town. The hamlet also does not have any provision of health centre; however, the people take shelter of private medical practitioners. In serious cases, they rush towards Akbarpur town or beyond. The hamlet is fully unelectrified. For drinking and other purposes the village people have got wells and hand-pipes. The wheat and barley are the main crops of the people of this area.

The residents are Hindus and speak Hindi. They believe in Hindu religious order and believe in deities like Shiva, Rama, Hanuman etc. Out of 30 families in hamlet, 22 families belong to Brahmin caste (Shukla—A Saryu Parin Brahmin). These Brahmins believe in Hinduism. In caste stratification, they had been using to enjoy highest prestigious position since antiquity not only within the hamlet but outside it also. They are comparatively big land owners and employ lower caste and untouchable caste members as their agricultural labourer or farm labourer. They still try to exercise the same prestigious power over the others falling lower to them in social stratification system of caste Hindu.

Caste Distribution in Hamlet

The hamlet consists of three castes. These are Brahmin, Kayastha and Bhar. Caste-wise distribution of population is shown below in Table 2.6.

Table 2.6

S. No.	*Castes*	*No. of Households*	*Percentage*
1.	Brahmin	22	73.33
2.	Kayastha	1	3.33
3.	Bhar	7	23.33
	Total	30	100.00

The table shows that Brahmins in the hamlet are in majority and Kayastha in minority. Bhar caste occupies the second place in hamlet. The Brahmins dominate the hamlet in socio-cultural and economic sphere. All the Brahmins are landowners and agriculturists. Some of them are in service in different private and government concerns. Out of 22 Brahmin households, there are 2 households who are in service. Out of the two servicemen, one serves in a private company at Delhi. There are another 6 Brahmin families in which some members are employed in different jobs in factories, military etc. These families have also owned a considerable size of land. A good size of land holding plus services in different concerns have made the Brahmins well-to-do. There is one Brahmin household head named Abhay Raj Shukla, one Brahmin household is both agriculturist and priest.

The house head of Kayastha family Mr. Nar Singh Lal Srivastava is agriculturist having 8 bighas of land and also he serves as Lekhpal. Out of 7 Bhar families, there are 6 families, who possess land between 1-2 bighas except one family who is landless labourer. The 6 families who have smallest size of land cultivate their own lands and also they work as agricultural and non-agricultural workers. These Bhar families do not work for Brahmin families of this hamlet but they go outside for earnings. They are united with the Bhars of village Ashraf Patti Newada and do not co-operate the Brahmins of Panjupur (Newada) for agricultural purposes.

Bahauddinpur—A Hamlet of Village Rabipur Bahauddinpur

The village Rabipur Bahauddinpur consists of 5 hamlets as mentioned in (census manuscript 1981) which are Sultanpur, Bahauddinpur, Rabipur, Chekhuri Ka Pura, and Lohar Ka Pura. Out of these 5 hamlets, Bahauddinpur has been selected for study as the relations among the castes of this hamlet have been viewed as more tensive.

Bahauddinpur is situated at the distance of 3 Kms. from Akbarpur town on Akbarpur-Tanda metalled road towards west. Railway route from Akbarpur to Tanda goes just from the east side of the hamlet. The hamlet accounts for a total population of 630 out of which males are 54.45% and females are 45.55%, the sex ratio being 6:5. Here, 11.55% of the total population are the literate males including educated also. The percentage of literate females is 1.21. Illiterate males are 42.94% while the percentage of illiterate opposite sex is 44.28.

There are four castes viz., Brahmin, Kayastha, Kurmi and Bhar. In all there are 97 families. 18 families are in Brahmin caste (Surname Pandey); 1 family in Kayastha (Surname) being Srivastava; 9 families in Kurmis (title being Verma); and 69 families in Bhar caste (title being Rajbhar).

The total occupied area is 170 acres out of which 138 acres of land is under cultivation.

The hamlet is fledged by a Primary School for the provision of imparting education to small children upto 5th standard. However, the children above this standard have to depend upon Akbarpur town for middle and higher education. There is no provision of medical amenity for the people of this area; however they can get all sorts of medical facilities at Akbarpur town where a primary health centre runs for the people of Akbarpur Tahsil. The hamlet is well equipped by wells and hand-pipes and the people enjoy them for drinking purposes. The number of wells and hand-pipes were counted by researcher himself and found that hand-pipes were in a considerable number (42); however the number of wells were only 8. Barley and wheat are the staple food of this area.

There are 264 persons belonging to different castes, engaged in different kinds of works. Some of them go at work in morning and come back in evening while there are others who have migrated to other distant cities and revisit the village after one or two years or so. Mostly agricultural and other like workers fall in former category who often work on daily wage while in second category fall those who work in different government concerns like Indian Railway, Telephone, P.W.D.

P.A.C., Defence, Irrigation, Forest, Hydel, Planning and so on, and also in well established private factories owned by industrialists. Out of 264, the number of persons engaged in agricultural work as agricultural labourer is 200. These labourers are Bhar by caste. They render most of their services to the persons of neighbouring villages. Rarely, they agree to render their services to some families of the hamlet. Out of 64 persons engaged in non-agricultural concerns, 9 persons work in different factories; 4 persons work in P.A.C. department; 2 persons are Military personnel; 28 are associated with the working of Gandhi Ashram; 5 are Postal employees; 1 works as Junior Engineer in tube-well department; 1 works as Junior Engineer in Hydel; 1 is Forest worker; 5 are engaged in P.W.D. activities. Planning department employs one person; Indian Railways provide job to 7 persons. Caste-wise distribution of these working personnel can be shown in Table 2.7.

The table shows that in comparison to other castes, Brahmins are more associated with force like P.A.C. and Defence. The factory workers among Bhar caste community figure more than that of Brahmin. The data regarding different occupations also show that Kurmis are less in number as non-agricultural cccupants as compared to Brahmins and Bhars. However, Kayastha being a single family has a better occupational position.

The listed households have been classified according to the caste and the family types they belong which have been exhibited in Table 2.8.

The table exhibits that the family jointness among Kurmis caste members is greater than Brahmin and Bhars. The Kayastha being a single family lives jointly though its some members reside at Faizabad city but they visit their native, the parent home if and when they feel to visit.

Hazipur Marui

Hazipur Marui which is a village of Akbarpur Tahsil falls at the distance of 8 kilometres from Akbarpur town on

Table 2.7

S. No.	*Caste*	*Factory Workers*	*P.A.C.*	*Defence*	*Gandhi Ashram*	*Postal Workers*	*Tube-well*	*Hydel*	*Forest*	*PWD*	*Planning*	*Rly.*	*Total*
1.	Brahmin (Pandey)	1	4	2	6	4	—	1	—	—	—	2	20
2.	Kayastha	—	—	—	—	—	1	—	—	—	—	—	1
3.	Kurmi	1	—	—	1	—	—	—	—	—	1	—	3
4.	Bhar	7	—	—	21	1	—	—	1	5	—	5	40
	Number of workers engaged in non-agricultural pursuits												64

Table 2.8

S. No.	Caste	Family Type		Total
		Joint	Nuclear	
1.	Brahmin	8	10	18
2.	Kayastha	1	—	1
3.	Kurmi	6	3	9
4.	Bhar	20	49	69
	Total	35	62	97

Akbarpur-Tanda Pucca Road. The total area of the village according to 1971 Census Part X B is 291 acres. The village is provided an educational institution of Junior Basic Stanoard. There is no medical amenity in the village; however, electricity is provided to the villagers. The village is well equipped by wells and hand-pipes which the villagers use for drinking purposes. Parallel to the village, there passes a pucca road at the distance of 2 kilometres which links Akbarpur and Tanda towns. Wheat and barley are the main staple foods of the villagers.

Out of 291 acres of total land, 85 acres of land are irrigated by canal, 40 acres of land are irrigated by wells and 60 acres of land are irrigated by tanks. Total number of irrigated land is 50. Cultivable waste figures 47 acres. The area not available for cultivation is 9 acres.

Census of 1971, Part X B reveals that in village Hazipur Marui, the total number of occupied residential houses is 80. Number of households is 90. The total population including institutional and houseless population figures 577 out of which male population figures 288 and female population figures 289. So far as scheduled caste population is concerned there are 88 males and 98 females. Data on literate and educated population are also shown in Census report of 1971, according to which males are 83 and females are 23. Total number of workers engaged in different pursuits is such that males are 153 while females do not represent this category. Out of these 153 male workers engaged in different occupational pursuits, 83 are owners and tenant cultivators. 48 are agricultural labourers. 15 persons are engaged in occupations other than industries. One individual works in wholesale or retail trading activity and commercial transaction relating to export and import. One individual villager works in transport activity by air, rail. The last category of workers belongs to public utility services (electricity, gas, water supply, sanitary services, central and state government employees, municipal employees, professional services). There are 5 workers in this category. Total number of non-workers is 424 out of which males are 135 and females are 289. The non-workers are those persons who do not do any productive work.

The total population of the village according to 1981 Census (unpublished) report obtained from the office of Tahsildar, Akbarpur is 639 out of which males are 301 and females are 338.

Although, village consists of two religious groups, viz., Hindus and Muslims but for the present study only Hindus have been selected. In Hindu population, there are many castes such as Kurmis, Lohar, Barhi, Loniya, Dhobi and Chamar but mainly there are two castes say Kurmi and Chamar in which conflict has been observed and measured. The bio-data of households of all the castes have been generated through an interview schedule which are needed to be analysed in different tables in order to understand the behaviour of these households (Table 2.9).

Total Number of Families of all Castes

The table shows that the number of families in Chamar caste is greatest and is 55.38% of the total families. Next comes Kurmi with 23.07% of the total. Other castes do not figure significantly (Table 2.10).

Table 2.9

Name of Caste Distribution in Village

S. No.	*Name of Caste*	*No. of Families*
1.	Kurmi	16
2.	Lohar	3
3.	Barhai	2
4.	Loniya	7
5.	Chamar	36
6.	Dhobi	2
	Total	65

Table 2.10

S. No.	*Caste*	*Land Holding (in Bighas)*	*No. of house heads*	*Total*	*Mean (a)*
1.	Kurmi	0- 5 5-10 10-15 15-20	8 4 1 2	15	6.5
2.	Dhobi	Less than 1	2	2	.5
3.	Barhai	2-4	2	2	3
4.	Lohar	2	3	3	2
5.	Loniya	0-1 1-3 3-5	2 4 1	7	1.86
6.	Chamar	0-1 1-3 3-6	18 16 2	36	1.39
	Total number of households in village				=65
	Average landholding of the households of all castes				=2.7

The table throws light on the fact that the average land holding of the Kurmi caste in the village is highest. Next comes Barhai. Lohar occupies third place. Lohiya is ranked fourth. Chamar occupies fifth place. Dhobi is the last in land rank-order.

3

Plans and Procedures

The two words tension and conflict are viewed as the synonym of the modern era. The whole globe ranging from family—the basic unit of the wider social world—to inter-nation seems to be eclipsed by the two. All the sectors of human activities are disturbed by one social factor or another.

The present study focusses its attention on inter-caste tension and conflict in rural society of Akbarpur Tehsil of Faizabad district. In this study, the main problem before the investigator was to identify the villages in which the tension between two or more castes was manifest. For this task, Block Development Officer of Akbarpur Block was first of all consulted who recommended on the basis of his own general observation some of the villages as victim of caste tension. Other sources used were public and a Revenue and Land-Record Keeper (Lekh Pal) who were very helpful in tracing out the villages. The investigator was surprised to know that in the view of public, almost all the villages were somewhat less or more the victim of caste tension. Keeping in mind the researcher's limitation, four villages from Akbarpur block were selected by the method of purposive sampling. The house-heads of different castes involved in tension and conflict being less in figure were selected by Census Method.

These house-heads (respondents) being almost illiterates were asked to reveal their response on the subject under study through a schedule. However, four cases were studied in deep to know the real scene of rural Hindu Caste Society.

Meanings of the Concepts Used

The Caste

The term "Caste" was derived from Portuguese word 'Casta' (meaning lineage or race) although in India the term Varna (meaning colour) is used as a synonym of caste. But, it is incorrect to call varna a caste. In Hindi, there are two different words, varna and jati, to denote two different types of groupings. To include both of them under a single term, caste, is erroneous, confusing and misleading.

The Varna system of Vedic times, according to authorities, was an open system. "Though the orthodox Hindu holds caste to be divine, caste was not known to the Rig Veda which did, however, distinguish between priests (Brahmans), nobles (Kshatriyas), tillers of the soil (Vaishyas), and slaves (Shudras)."[1] During that period though "the functions were regarded as hereditary, exceptions were freely allowed. The Brahmans had the possibilities of a warrior. The crisis of old were agriculturists and sometimes warriors too."[2] Similarly, the "... Kshatriyas were frequent by adding to their numbers both from foreign in-coming elements and others in country who rose to power and authority."[3] Durant has clearly stated that the "first caste division was not by status but by colour. Among the Aryans themselves marriage (except of near kin) was free and status was not defined by birth."[4]

1. Don, Martindale, *Social Life and Cultural Change*, D. Van Nostrand Co., Princeton, 1962, p. 180.
2. S. Radhakrishnan, *The Hindu View of Life*, George Allen and Unwin Ltd., London, 1954, p. 112.
3. Jawahar Lal Nehru, *The Discovery of India*, Meridian Books Ltd., London, 1956, p. 249.
4. Will Durant, *The Story of Civilisation*, (Part One) (Our Oriental Heritage), Simon and Schuster, New York, 1954, p. 398.

Although "the classes had come to be almost stereotyped by the end of the Vedic period, but it was not altogether impossible for an upward and downward change to occur....."[1] Historical evidence suggests that several Kshatriya Kings became Brahmans by giving up certain practices and by adopting certain others. "According to 'Harivansha' Purana, two sons of Nabhgarishta, who were Vaishyas, became Brahmans. Even Shudras seem sometimes to have become Brahmans...."[2] "The whole of the Kshatriyas varna is claimed by Brahmans to have been extirpated by Parasurama, but if so it has been replaced by manufactured Kshatriyas."[3] Bougle asserts that "it will be useless to look at the castes of the present as the descendants of the four traditional castes."[4]

Although the main objective of this study is not to understand or identify the caste in empirical setting but to understand interpersonal relations among different castes of Hindu society in rural areas. I would like to begin with Yogesh Atal's work[5] on *The Changing Frontiers of Caste* (1968) who has done a pioneering work in this field. He has reviewed twenty three definitions of caste attempted by different scholars which have been classified into three main categories viz., caste as a group, caste as a social system and combined definitions of these two. The areas of confusion are (i) Varna and Caste; and (ii) Caste and Sub-Caste.

On the basis of hierarchy of attributes for the caste as unit and the caste as a system can be arranged as under:

1. G.S. Ghurye, *Caste and Class in India*, Popular Book Depot, Bombay, 1957, p. 45.
2. J.H. Hutton, *Caste in India*, Oxford University Press, Bombay, 1961, p. 65.
3. Ibid., p. 67.
4. C. Bougle, "The Essence and Reality of the Caste System", *Contribution to Indian Sociology*, Vol. II, 1958, p. 28.
5. Yogesh Atal, *The Changing Frontiers of Caste*, National Publishing House, Delhi, 1968, p. 14.

(a) Caste as a Unit:

1. Basic (Pivotal) attributes: Endogamy
2. Sufficiently relevant attributes:
   (i) membership by birth
   (ii) common occupation
   (iii) Caste council.
3. Peripheral attributes:
   (i) Name
   (ii) Diacritical sign.

(b) Caste as a system:

The attributes that characterize the caste system may be arranged as follows:

1. Basic attribute: Plurality of interacting endogamous groups.
2. Sufficiently relevant attribute: Hierarchy.
3. Peripheral attribute: Traditional division of labour.

If we consider caste as a unit, it may, in the light of above, be defined as an endogamous social group having a definite set of rules called council to control over the individual members who are ascribed a permanent status on the basis of birth, having a common occupation, a particular name and whose members bear a particular life style.

To understand individual castes, it is essential to understand caste as a unit and this definition shall be of great help. But it is not merely enough to understand caste as unit, to understand caste, it is also crucial to know the system i.e., caste as a social system. To define caste as a social system it is precise to imagine a hierarchically arranged endogamous social group in which all the constituent groups are attributed by a traditional occupation.

Tension and Conflict

Tension has been widely used as a psychological construct, its precise nature and its physiological and psychological properties are far from clear. Ghurye[1] points out that "tension is a state of mind which renders the group or a member of the group, which is the cause of tension, obnoxious and tends to evoke a pattern of behaviour which may be marked by or compounded of the below stated attitudes viz., "Humility", "Snobbishness", "Patronage", "Arrogance", "Scorn", "Aversion", "Spitefulness", and "Suspiciousness", etc." The definition of tension given by Ghurye is purely a psychological as he looks tension as a state of mind which leads to a pattern of behaviour which is marked by or compounded of different negative attitudes like arrogance, aversion, spitefulness, scorn etc. This is the psycho-operational definition of what we call tension and it does not serve the purpose of our study. Although these attitudes of individuals or groups towards other individuals or groups can be taken into account as indicators of tension for a social psychologist. A physio-psychological study has been conducted by Clement[2] who sees tension as the manifestation of the universal intermolecular force that is observed in the surface of fluids. Drives or organic cravings which are the original motive powers for activity originate in various segments of the automatic nervous system. When one of them begins to operate, tension accumulates in particular segments of the system and causes restlessness and random activity till it is created by appropriate activity.

Some studies which seem to be sociologically relevant are by Professor Dobree[3] and Trevelyan.[4] Prof. Dobree highlights that the tension is due to social and economic changes bursting forth into organized violence. He himself writes that the peasant's revolt and the chartist violence were

1. G.S. Ghurye, *Social Tensions in India*, Popular Prakashan, Bombay, 1968, p. 2.
2. John A. Clement, *Scientific American* in G.S. Ghurye, *Social Tensions in India*, 1968, p. 4.
3. Bonamy Dobree, The English Revolt in G.S. Ghurye, Ibid, p. 4.
4. G.M. Trevelyan, *English Social History*, in G.S. Ghurye, Ibid., p. 3.

consequence of the "emotions bred in the hearts of those who were oppressed and frustrated of food and freedom." Trevelyan also points out that the causes of tension are social and economic grievances.

A psychological study has been undertaken by Lewin[1] who developed a system of social psychology generally known as "Field Theory" but may be termed as Tensional Psychology also. He speaks "System of Tensions" within the individual and separates the "Pressure emanating from the environment", i.e., the individual's motives depending upon group pressure, speaking of the two together as "Field Forces" which has given the common label "Field Theory" to his psychological contribution.

Apart from these definitions covering physio-psychological areas, I shall cite some other definitions relevant for understanding tension and conflict altogether as social realities and they shall be the basic guiding lines for the present research purpose.

International Encyclopaedia of Social Sciences[2] (No. 3 and 4) defines social conflict as a struggle over values or claims to status, power, and scarce resources, in which the aims of conflicting parties are not only to gain the desired values but also to neutralize, injure, or eliminate their rivals. Such conflicts may take place between individuals, between collectivities, or between individuals and collectivities. Intergroup as well as intra-group conflicts are perennial features of social life.

Conflict is an important element of social interaction. Far from being always a "negative" factor that "tears apart", social conflict may contribute many ways to the maintenance of groups and collectivities as well as to the cementing of interpersonal relations.

1. Kurt Lewin, *Resolving Social Conflict*, Harper Brothers Publishers, New York, 1948, p. 9.
2. *International Encyclopaedia of Social Sciences*, No. 3 and 4.

Dahrendorf[1] also rightly points out that conflict is "the struggle among groups over ideology or way of life or over power or scarce values, which can be explained in terms of patterns of social structure."

Conflict between religious or caste groups is called as ideological conflict.[2] Groups possessing distinct set of values and opposing each other for the maintenance of these values can be considered as engaged in *ideological conflict.* This difference in ways of life constitutes the source or base of conflict. But the area of conflict may extend beyond the realm of these values. Though the groups are formed on the basis of distinct values, they tend to oppose each other in all spheres, thereby making it necessary for the total involvement of members in the group conflict. The conflict may primarily be on the basis of different values held by the opposing groups. But it may extend to political, economic and social spheres.[3]

Methods of the Study

Techniques

For the collection of data, four techniques have been used. They are: (i) Observation; (ii) Schedule containing 34 questions in common and 18 and 20 questions for respectively higher and lower castes separately. Schedule is the name usually applied to a set of questions which are asked and filled in by an interviewer in a face to face situation with another person.[4] (iii) Group interview. This technique as experienced by researcher himself was found to be very useful in collection of field data. It is meritorious in the sense that it takes least

1. Ralf Dahrendorf, *Class and Class Conflict in Industrial Society*, Routledge and Kegan Paul Ltd., London, 1959, p. 238.
2. G. Ramchandra Raj, *Functions and Dysfunctions of Social Conflict*, Popular Prakashan, Bombay, 1974, p. 5.
3. William J. Goode and Paul K. Hatt, *Methods in Social Research Ltd.*, 1952, p. 132.
4. Ibid.

time and generates more information concerning the study; and (iv) Case study.

Case Study

A comprehensive study of a social unit—be that unit a person, a group, a social institution, a district or a community —is called a case study.[1]

Universe

Four villages from Akbarpur block were selected purposively to understand the pattern of caste conflict. They are: (i) Panjupur (Newada); (ii) Ashrafpati (Newada) (iii) Rabipur Bahauddinpur; and (iv) Hazipur Marui.

Respondents

In the study of pattern of caste conflict, only those castes were considered who were involved in conflict. The families of those castes were less in number. Therefore, all the house-heads of the castes involved in conflict were selected for the study. Here, it is mentioned that the method of selection of respondents is census. Some house-heads who were out of station and have gone at too distant places to earn money were automatically left uninterviewed.

Pre-testing

First of all, schedule was framed tentatively on the basis of existing and available sociological literature and own experience. This schedule was then tested on some house-heads of the villages. While asking the questions from respondents, the researcher realized many drawbacks in the schedule. During this period, other books relevant to the study were read. The data which the schedule was measuring seemed to be futile. Many questions seemed to be unnecessary.

1. P.V. Young, *Scientific Social Survey and Research*, Prentice Hall of India Pvt. Ltd., New Delhi, 1975, p. 247.

Therefore, unuseful questions were replaced and a somewhat new schedule was constructed which was proved to be alright then. The researcher then proceeded to field again to contact with the hon'ble respondents—the nucleus of the study, and urged for co-operation. This is in this context worth recording that the respondents were giving their responses very sympathetically and politely in a free, frank and fearless manner.

The data collected were not tabulated immediately but they were processed and edited, and possible errors and internal contradictions were removed.

Variables

For the purpose of the present study four variables have been taken into account on which the data on 200 respondents, as and where it was felt necessary, have been tabulated. These are caste, age, education, and family type. The researcher started the tabulation work by the method of 'Tally-Mark' and a huge master chart was prepared. The different tables were formed and the responses were calculated in class as well as in total percentages in order to make a clear-cut comparison. In few questions, the responses were more than two and hence, they needed some specific codes. A separate code-manual was prepared which was very helpful in showing the data in shortest space. While interpreting for the tables containing codes the code-manual served as a very useful device in decoding such codes (Table 3.1).

The table shows that the universe of respondents contains in it 18.5% of Brahman respondents. The Kurmi respondents show a per cent of 11.5. The respondents belonging to Bhar caste constitute 53% which is the greatest of all. However, Chamar respondents show 17%.

The table also shows that the Bhar respondents are

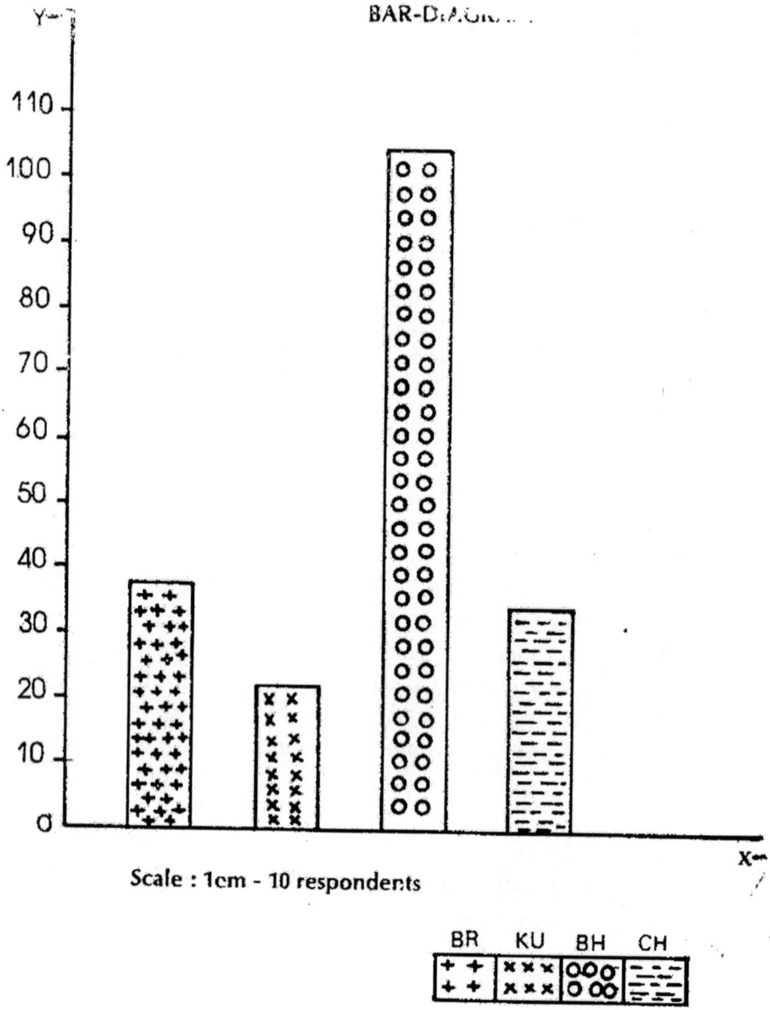

Caste status of the Respondents shown in Bar-diagram

Table 3.1

Caste Status of Respondents

Respondents	*Number*	*Percentage*
Brahman	37	18.5
Kurmi	23	11.5
Bhar	106	53
Chamar	34	17
Total	200	100.0

maximum and Kurmi respondents are minimum. Brahmans occupy the second place while Chamars the third.

Table 3.2

Age of the Respondents

Age of the respondents (in years)	*Number*	*Percentage*
15–25	7	3.5
25–35	41	20.5
35–45	56	28
45–55	35	17.5
55–65	38	19
65–75	16	8
75–85	7	3.5
Total	200	100.0

Mean age a=46.1 years

The table shows that the age group 35-45 is the modal age group in the sense that it contains maximum frequency of the respondents (28%). The mean age of the respondents is 46.1 and modal age is 38.66.

ANGULAR DIAGRAM

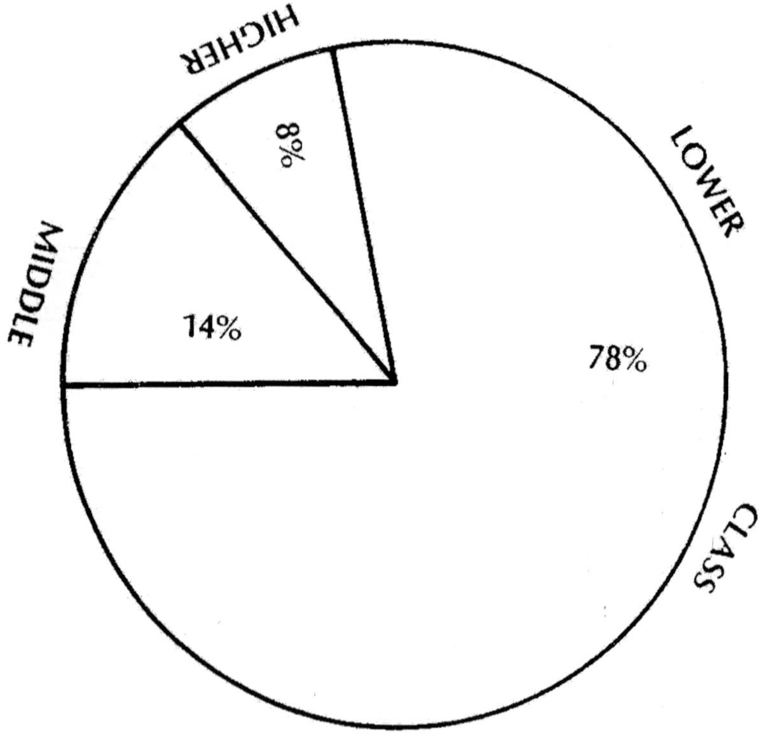

Educational status of the respondents shown il Angular diagram

The percentages of the respondents are as such 3.5% of respondents belong to age group 15-25. 20.5% belong to 25-35. 28% of respondents lie in age group 35-45. 45-55 age group shows 17.5% of respondents. Age group 55-65 contains 19%,. 65-75 contains 8% while age group 75-85 contains 3.5% of respondents.

Table 3.3

Educational Status of the Respondents

Education of Respondents	*Number*	*Percentage*
Illiterates	119	59.5
Nominally Educated	78	39
Highly Educated	3	1.5
Total	200	100.0

The table indicates that more than half of the total respondents (59.5%) in our universe are illiterates. Here, illiterates are those who have no educational background nor can they read the letters nor write the letters. 39% of respondents are nominally educated. Nominally educated respondents are those who are at least literates. In this category, the respondents having upto Intermediate qualification have been included. Last category is the category of highly educated respondents. The respondents having at least Bachelor's degree and above have been considered as highly educated. 1.5% of respondents in our universe are highly educated.

Table 3.4 shows that most of our respondents (78%) belong to lower income bracket. The middle class of the respondents constitute 14% while higher class of the respondents being least in number show a percentage of 8 only.

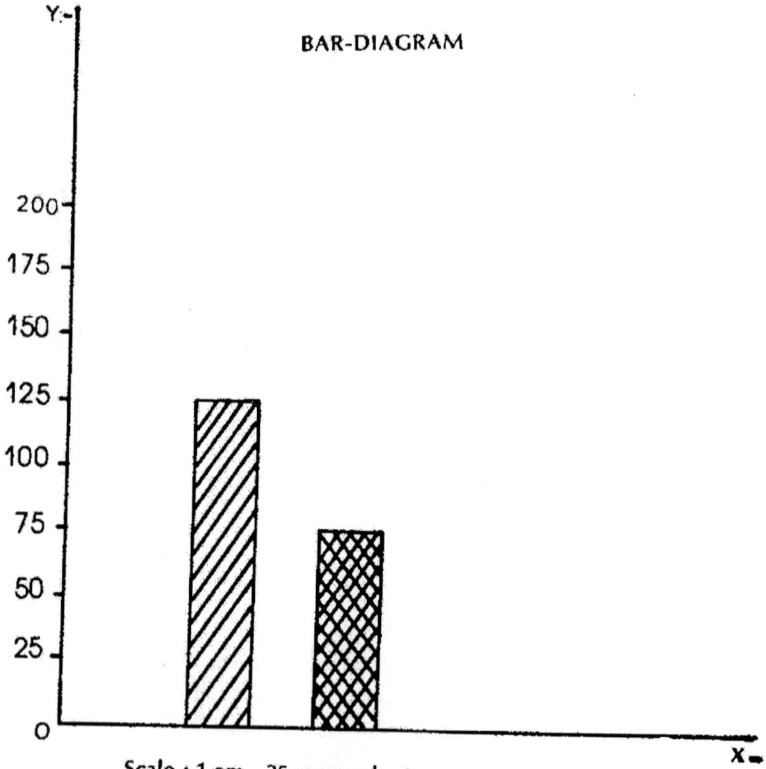

Scale : 1 cm - 25 respondents

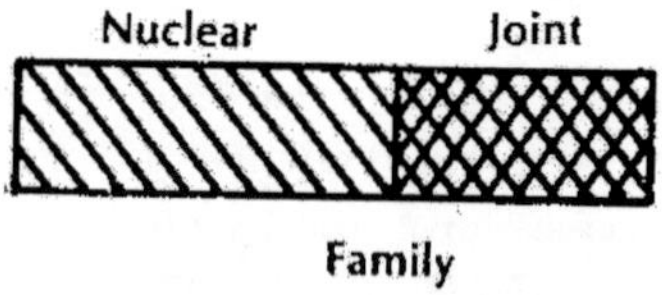

Family types of the respondents shown in Bar-diagram

Table 3.4

Economic Status of the Respondents

Income per month (In Rupees)	*Number*	*Percentage*
0–500 (Lower)	156	29
500–1000 (Middle)	28	14
1000 and above (Higher)	16	8

Mean income Rs. 400.00

The mean or average income of the respondents is approximately Rs. 400 per month, which throws light on the fact that the poverty in general prevails in villages still today and most of the village people are below poverty line. Only a few enjoy a prosperous life.

Table 3.5

Respondents and their Family Types

Family Type	*Number*	*Percentage*
Nuclear	125	62.5
Joint	75	37.5
Total	200	100.0

The table shows that 62.5% of respondents in our universe belong to nuclear family and 37.5% of respondents belong to joint family. The percentage of respondents belonging to nuclear family is much greater than those who belong to joint family.

4

Emergence of Caste Conflict

(A Historical Context)

The history of conflict is as old as the history of human evolution. Truly, human race has since ever been struggling hard for its existence. Every age has been the age of struggle, conflict and crisis. May that age be the age of human civilization or agricultural, primitive or modern. In every age and at every point of time, a direct correlation between man and conflict has been explicitly viewed. In all ages of human civilization, it is universally factual and widely acceptable that conflict and human evolution have always gone parallel to each other. Today, the whole cosmos of mankind seems to be burning in rampant fire of conflict. The trinity of the clash of interests between individuals or groups, the rampant desire of gaining power, and the extreme want to lead a prestigious social position, has severely dashed every individual from other individuals distant, creating a deeper gulf which is a matter of great curiosity, anxiety and serious thought.

To understand conflict from sociological point of view, the researcher has picked up Indian caste system. It is here desired to see conflict inherent in somewhat less or more degree in Indian caste system through ages. If India's caste system is the defective or twisted form of its varna system, we view the fundamentals of conflict seeded in its very root. Here, it is contextual to find out the prevailing elements of conflict present in inter-personal relationship of the structural components of Varna order. These components are Brahman, Kshatriya, Vaishya and Shudra.

F. Max Muller has described the gravity of Brahmans in a systematic manner in his world fame book entitled *The Sacred Books of the East* which can be mentioned as under :

Man is said to be purer above his novel than below, therefore, the self-existent (Swayambhu) has declared it as His purest organ (face).[1]

Since, Brahman has originated from the mouth of Brahma, and since he is elder and authority of Vedas, and therefore, he is master of whole creation.[2] Because, self-existent, after the total subsistence, created him from his mouth, so that the sacrificial things might be conveyed to Gods, and worldly men and world as a whole might be given protection.[3] Who can dare to avoid him through whose mouth, the Gods themselves continuously consume the sacrificial things, and tell the things offered to dead bodies as the feast of forefathers.[4] The birth of Brahman is, then, an external incarnation of holy law to provide protection to the property of God, and he disappears alongwith the disappearance of Brahma.[5] When a Brahman comes into existence, he takes birth upon the earth as a super-human and highest and as a master of all the creatures.[6] Whatever exists in the universe, that is all the property of Brahman being supermost since birth. Of course, Brahman is the authority of all these

1. F. Max Muller, *The Sacred Books of the East* (ed.) quoted in N. Prasad, Jati Vyavastha, Raj Kamal Prakashan, Delhi, 1965, p. 19.
2. Loc. Cit.
3. Loc. Cit.
4. Loc. Cit.
5. Loc. Cit.
6. Loc. Cit.

things.[1] A Brahman, whether he is idle or learned, is a master of a great excellence just like fire.[2]

The provision of punishment for Brahman in Varna system was as follows :

To ensure ceremony is most appropriate for Brahmans in the place of capital punishment. But other Varnas shall have to accept capital punishment.[3] No Brahman should be killed in any condition irrespective of his numerous crime commitments. Such Brahman criminal should be exiled and his whole property should be allowed to be with him and his body should not be tortured.[4] No more severe crime is known on the earth than to kill a Brahman. So, a king should not and may not even think mentally to kill a Brahman.[5]

The birth of Shudras for enslavement

But a Shudra, whether purchased or not, can be forcibly pressed to work as a slave, because self-existent has himself created a Shudra to be slave of Brahmans. A Shudra, even after getting rid of his master, cannot get rid of slavery. Because, slavery is associated with his birth. Who can allow him to be free from that ? A Brahman, after being assured, may capture the property of his slave (Shudra), because a Shudra (slave) has no right to possess property. His master may have right over his existence.

To serve Brahmans is the only means of livelihood declared for Shudras, because whatever a Shudra shall do other than service to Brahmans, this shall all be fruitless.[6] Shudras, even after being capable to accumulate the wealth,

1. Loc. Cit.
2. Loc. Cit.
3. Loc. Cit.
4. Ibid., pp. 19-20.
5. Ibid., p. 20.
6. Loc. Cit.

should never do so. Because the prosperous or wealthy Shudra aggrieves the Brahmans.[1]

The Award of Slavery

They should certainly provide the Shudras enough for their livelihood and for the livelihood of his family and this should be done, for which he is bound, only after a careful examination and consideration of his capacity, labour and number.[2] He must be given food defiled by eating and also old cloths, the remains of grains etc.

Penal system for Shudras

If a Shudra uses abusive languages to assault a dwij (Brahman), his tongue shall be cut and shall be separated from body, because he belongs to low family. If he calls the name of a dwij or mentions his caste with disrespect, a burning iron nail whose length is equivalent to breadth of ten fingers (ten anguls long) would be poured into his mouth.[3]

If he preaches the Brahmans of their duties, the king would arrange hot oil to pour into his mouth and ears. If the low varna person, whether why not by any organ of his body, tortures the higher varnas, his that organ shall be cut.[4] This is the preaching of Manu. He who uses his hand or stick for this purpose, his hand shall be damaged; he who aggressively kicks out by his leg, his leg shall be cut. If a low varna person tries to substitute himself at the place of a Brahman, his hip shall be branded by hot iron and he shall be exiled, or the king shall make an arrangement to make a deeper wound at his hip. If he spits at a person superior to him due to pride, the king shall make an arrangement to cut his both the lips. If he makes water at him, his penis; !f he discharges polluted

1. Ibid., p. 21.
2. Loc. Cit.
3. Loc. Cit.
4 Ibid., p. 22.

air before him, his 'guda' shall be cut. If he snatches the hairs of a higher varna, the king ought to cut his hand without hitch. Similarly, if he touches the Brahman's feet with scribbling, then his beard, neck or 'andkos.'[1]

The prescribed standard of behaviour for some Varnas:[2]

The residence of Chandals and Shwapakis shall be out of village. They shall be disabled and dogs and mules shall be the only wealth of theirs. Their cloths shall be cadavour-like dress. They shall eat in broken dish. The black iron shall be their ornaments, and they shall necessarily move from one place to another.[3]

A Shudra shall not commit such a crime less his race should go to extinction. He shall not enjoy holy religious texts. He has no right to follow the rules of rituals, even then, he is not prohibited to follow some parts of Aryan cult. Therefore, a Shudra should not be given an advice. Neither he should be given the remains of food-stuff, nor the offerings to God (Prasad), nor religious explanation before him, nor provision of penance. He who puts the explanation of religious rules before a Shudra shall also drown in hell known as Asamvrit.[4]

The provision of penance in case a person kills a Shudra :[5]

Any person who kills a Shudra may practice penance of his sin by killing a cat, a mongoose, a magpie, a frog, a dog, a lizard, an owl, or a crow.[6]

Through the analysis of the facts mentioned above, it reveals that the social status of Brahmans in India's varna

1. Loc. Cit.
2. Loc. Cit.
3. Ibid., p. 22.
4. Loc. Cit.
5. Loc. Cit.
6. Loc. Cit.

system was highest and that of Shudras, the lowest. Warriors or Kings (Kshatriyas) were working under the direction of Brahmans. In this way, Brahmans worked as pressure group. In Varna system, where, on one hand, one finds division of labour and as a consequence the emergence of group of experts (specialists), on the other hand, the tendency of exploitation rooted in the system is found. In this reference, Davis's work may be cited who mentioned that inequality exists in a society due to unequal distribution of power, prestige and rewards.[1] To deprive the Shudras of social, economic, political and cultural provisions is certainly in-human. This is undoubtedly true that in such a system, the Shudras might have been frustrated and had felt a sense of social insecurity and injustice. But, why did they not fight against Brahmans in past can best be explained and argued in ways said below. It is and it may be that Shudras had no education and, therefore, had no consciousness and hence, they were uncapable of raising their voices of deprivation of values against Brahmans. Secondly, there was the provision of severe penal system for Shudras and therefore no Shudra dared to react against any Brahman or Kshatriya. Thirdly, even Kshatriyas (King) were controlled, directed, regulated and conducted by Brahmans. The Brahman Varna as a whole because of his intelligence and spiritual power and command over all sorts of knowledge related to every aspect of human race was easily able to exercise his power over all other varnas. The analysis of all these facts does not contain in itself the denial of non-existence of elements of revenge and conflict in the system. They were of course seeded in the system-ground but were not in the process of evolution. The seeds of conflict were depressed, oppressed and suppressed by the heavy and polluted storm of established codes of conduct. It is true that evolution has a direct link with environment. A seed can never grow in absence of proper environment. A particular human behaviour is directly proportional to time and space. As the time and space vary, human behaviour also varies. Underground seed if unevolved becomes rotten. Similarly, the seed of conflict

1. Kingsley Davis, *Human Society*, The Macmillan Company, New York, 1969, pp. 373-74.

which could never emerge in classical India is diffusing today due to numerous of changes brought by legal legislations enacted by Government of India. Today, India Government is committed to establish democratic values based on equality, fraternity, and justice before law. Today, political institutions have come into existence to fight against injustice made towards any individual, caste, varna, creed or tribe.

Due to spread of education and provision of eradication of mass illiteracy through adult education scheme; economic growth of lower castes and lower classes; industrialization; urbanization; occupational mobility; the special provision of reservation of seats to backwards, and scheduled castes including scheduled tribes, social security measures; and untouchability removal act have made the untouchables and lower caste people to form organization. Now, they have awaken to fight against injustice. They darely put forth their problems. They now do not fear from higher castes. Today, the whole India's scene is surrounded by factionalism, casteism, caste conflict and class conflict within caste system.

Brahmans since tradition have been religiously trust worthy and only because of their such prejudiced religious staunchness, the conflict on large scale between Brahmanism and revolutionary movements like Buddhism and Jainism was obviously seen in medieval India, and Buddhism was defeated for ever. In this period, after the establishment of Moghul imperialism, where on one hand the Indian Hindus were undergoing conversion in Islamic religion, on the other hand, unadaptive Hindu religious staunchness was firmly standing forth. Numerous of religious social reformers tried their best to reduce the width and breadth of the gulf between the two conflicting religious groups through the process of negotiation, but India's low castes used to undergo Islamic conversion only so as to be free from grievances caused by higher castes. This is the reason why Buddhism had been people's religion and it remained, maintained and continued for thousands of years. Likely, in Moghul period, the Indian people began to adopt Islamic style of religion through conversion only because Islam provided them social equality and opportunities to enhance their social status in the world. But being alert from this dangerous siren, some social reformers tried to bring out change in social structure of Hindus. The first attempt of this reform was 'Vir Shiva movement' which aimed at ending the caste system and removing other social restraints.[1] The pioneer of this movement was a Brahman named Basava, as a consequence of whose efforts the people broke the barriers of caste rules and established marriage relations between Brahmans and Chandals. Basava widely propagated the gravity and essentiality of hard work. In his leadership, Lingayat sect came into existence who fought against priests to end the importance of temples and statue-worship.

Some words of Basava seem to be full of modern revolutionary emotions which are as under :

> What is the use of listening to Shastras and Puranas? Of what use is it to us if we read the Vedas and Vettantas ?
>
> May I admit the greatness of the Shastras ? It enforces Karma. May I regard the Vedas as important ? They advise slaughter of animals.
>
> The Adipurana tells only of Asuras; the Veda Purana resorts to the slaughter of goats; Ramayan speaks only of demons (Rakshasas); the Mahabharata relates family feuds. All these Puranas preach Karma first; but your Purana is matchless, O Lord Kudala Sangama.[2]

Furthermore :

> Those who are well versed in the Veda, Shastra, Purana, Agama etc. are not great. A rope-dancer is a master of

1. S.K. Ayyangar, *Some Contributions of South India to Indian Culture* in N. Prasad, *Jati Vyvastha*, 1965, p. 49.
2. S.M. Hunashal, *The Lingayat Movement*, Karnatak Sahitya Mandir, Dharwar, 1947, p. 99.

> sixty four lores. Is he then inferior ? This is not the right criterion. It is quite different. All these are bread earning lores; therefore he is great who has realized vurtya, knowledge and religious conduct and purity. . . .[1]

A Brahmin is not born to read the Veda and the Shastra :

> A Kshatriya is not meant to kill and be merry,
> Trading is not the monopoly of Vaishya;
> Our god Kama Bhima does not consent without
> Examining the merits and demerits of a farmer.

Basava preached the men to lead their lives through labour and hard work. His preachings were propagated at large scale among the traders and peasants of Karnatak. Today, Lingayats have got their separate social identity as a caste. They have got their own style of life. Their priests are just like Brahmans of staunch Hindu society.

Another reform-oriented movement also started from south and diffused in whole India which is universally known as 'Vaishnava movement'. The followers of this movement believe in salvation through Bhakti. The movement refused the significance of caste barriers and raised its voice against inequality between males and females. The pioneers of this movement in north India were Rama Nand and Kabir who was the son of a Muslim weaver. Besides these, the names of Dadu, Nanak and Nam Deo are also associated with this movement. Ultimately comes Chaitanya Deo of Bengal. The movement propounded by Chaitanya Deo was accelerated and pushed forth as a reform-oriented movement by Nitya Nand and his son Vir Chand. This movement, in social aspect of human life, was competitor of Islam. Afterwards, a group emerged as a consequence of the movement which was called as 'Jati Vaishnava'. Even today, any person belonging to any caste may become the member of this group after taking the prescribed education and initiation. This group (Jati-

1. Ibid., p. 96.

Vaishnava) has disrupted the caste-discrimination. Still today, it is an orphanage for those who are socially depressed and boycotted.[1]

Although, the objectives of these reform-oriented movements were to end caste discriminations but their social consequences were that the different movements formed their separate castes. Some of them claimed themselves to be Brahman, for example, Nath-sect. Later on, all these sects separately became endogamous social groups and they all became the victim of Brahmanic cult. Of course, after time-interval, the Brahman cult again became so dominant that without accepting the Brahmanic rules and ways it was impossible to achieve social prestige.

In modern India even, numerous of reform-oriented movements have been started in Hindu society and surprising changes have taken place in many aspects of India's social life. An example of M.K. Gandhi, the father of Indian nation, may be cited in this regard, who started 'Harijan movement' in order to enhance the socio-economic conditions of untouchables, but unfortunately this movement too became a caste organization. Consequently, backward castes also got their own caste organizations as well as the organization of amalgamation of analogous castes.

From these facts, we may pass a concluding remark that caste-patriotism and casteism in India are more prevalent than nationalism and this reality is a threat and challenge to Indian national integration.

Caste in British India

Before the introduction of Britishers in India, it was clearly observed that the jurisdictions of the states were scattered, every region (Ilaka) of a Chief or King remained

1. B.N. Dutta, *Studies in Indian Social Polity*, Quoted in N. Prasad, op. cit., p. 48.

separate from each other Generally, there was emperor himself or his subedar above such chiefs and below them remained sardars. The jurisdictions or limits of regions of chiefs were always changing. This change in jurisdiction depended upon the armed force of chiefs or kings and also upon the fact as to how firmly did emperor control over chiefs. Although, these jurisdictions used to change in time range, they created cleavages between the people of different states under the control of individual chiefs or kings. Hence, naturally such type of political system firmly checked the horizontal extension of caste-relations. In short, it can be stated that the political limits were determinant of some effective social extension, if not more, of every caste residing in the same region.[1] In a particular situation, these limits used to change. The meaning of this fact is that the cultural ties were frequently breaking across the existing political limits of that time.

The natural consequence of such political system which checked the tendency of horizontal extension of castes was that numerous of castes living in a particular region were intuited to cooperate each other. The occupational specialization of different castes also bound them to be inter-dependent as every caste depended upon other caste for its livelihood. Further, all the members of every caste were desirous of availing services, facilities, and advantages rendered by other castes; and it is clearly meant that there was antagonism in social relationship among members of a caste. This tendency of economic ties which cut across the caste barriers was supported by political and economic barriers. After the establishment of British imperialism, the castes became free from those bounds.

Due to construction of roads in whole India, introduction of communication such as Railway, Post and Telegraphs,

1. E.J. Miller, *Village Structure in North Kerala*, (ed) in M.N. Srivastava, *India's Villages*, Asia Publishing House, Bombay, 1960, p. 46.

cheap papers and printing press specially in local or regional languages, there emerged many caste organizations which were never so in past. The news of meetings (baithak) of caste-organization were communicated to the castemen spread at distant places through a post-card and when they felt necessity they assembled at a place from distant villages by train. Due to publication and easy availability of cheap newspapers, it was very simple and easy task to maintain, write, publish and send 'caste-journals'. The main objective of these journals was to encourage the interests of own castes. Generally, it is narrated that Railways and factories have weakened the food restrictions and rules of social intercourse but this argument is biased and exparte. Availability of papers on cheap rates counted much in writing caste disputes due to which rules, laws, and constitution, and old matters got permanent shape, which, in past, depended only upon the memory of old persons and which could be challenged at any time in case the same was forgotten by some persons. Many castes of Gujarat province have got their caste-constitutions published.

The impact of English empires on Indian caste system has been intellectually interpreted by eminent Professor Dr. Govind Sadashiva Ghurye[1] in the light of which the disruption in caste system in modern India, anomie, and tension may be clearly viewed and understood. Most of the people suppose that the major portion of authorities and powers which were conferred to caste Panchayats before the implementation of civil and penal codes by British Raj in Indian peninsula, became inherent in these codes. British authorities maintained a distinction between secular and religious matters.[2] In former, British principles of equal opportunity and equality before law were to be applied. Religious matters were to be left to traditional authorities. The principles

1. G.S. Ghurye, *Ccste and Class in India*, Popular Prakashan, Bombay, 1952.
2. For detailed study, please see the article of M. Glen and Sipra Bose Johnson on "Social Mobility among Untouchables" in Giri Raj Gupta, *Cohesion and Conflict in Modern India*, Vikas Publishing House Pvt. Ltd., New Delhi, 1978, pp. 60-95.

of equality before law irrespective of caste were enjoyed by some peasants through judiciary but it does not mean that village/caste panchayat have lost their importance in rural India. Really, these two institutions have significant role in the solution of rural problems today also. It is true that British Raj have established and developed economic forces in the country, and consequently the traditional caste hierarchy has certainly been observed disrupted, but it is never meant that casteism has weakened. Surely, lower caste people have got opportunities to change their traditional occupations and earn more money but when they tried to claim their social status higher than other traditionally superior castes, they were opposed. Furthermore, when such claim of lower castes was accepted by higher or other castes, the intensity of opposition did not reduce. Instead of urging for an end of existing caste system, the lower caste new bourgeoisie always made frequent efforts that they might attain higher social status and people might recognize and welcome them.

There was the provision of mentioning caste of all individuals in 'Ten-Year Census' by the English, which encouraged social mobility. As a consequence the lower castes rich as well as poor persons began to address themselves by new and highly Sanskritized names. Therefore, the 'Ten-Year Census' propounded by the British Raj may be viewed as a part of movement in the direction of 'higher-status-achievement' by lower caste people. The British Raj, from time to time, tried its best to provide financial assistance to the poor castes, but its benefit generally went to higher caste persons. Setting some defiled and degraded occupations aside, in almost all sectors of economic action, the higher caste persons were benefited. The Western education gave them ample opportunity to enter these sectors and the higher castes such as Brahmans, Vaishyas and Kayasthas were benefited of these opportunities upto maximum. Those castes whose socio-economic position was pre-dominant became doctors, engineers teachers, officers, lawyers and clerks. The Vaishyas availed the maximum commercial facilities provided by the British. In the then period, a new class of intellectuals comprising of these three castes emerged which took the complete responsibility of Indian National Movement on their shoulders. The higher caste persons were full of sentiments of nationalism, but they were also quite familiar with this fact that they were Hindus first. Specially Brahmans were more cautious and conscious towards this fact as they were highly privileged in traditional caste-hierarchy, and were enjoying special authority.

Where, on one hand, the matter of providing priority to lower caste people by the British was humanitarian, on the other hand, its social impact was that the lower castes began to attract and orient towards the Britishers and cleavage between higher and lower castes was observed, which was specially manifest in Indian sub-peninsula.

Prof. Ghurye has written that Brahmans and Rajputs were mainly the model castes with highest frequency in Bengal defence before Indian Revolt of 1857 and they specially played pioneering role in the creation of revolt. Immediately after this, the idea in England was more emphasized that the high-caste personnel should be expelled out of defence. A commission was established under the headship of Lord Peal to reorganize India's defence in which statements were generated from high rank holding English authorities. After the collection of information, it was proposed to appoint the soldiers of different castes in inland Indian defence. It was also proposed that the different caste soldiers might generally be kept commingled, in each and every regiment. Just after it, the number of higher caste persons began to lower down gradually. Ghurye mentions that by this revolt, the English administrators began to realize the fact that it is essential to divide Indian people on the basis of caste in order to persist and maintain the smooth functioning of British Raj. The fact that Indian society was divided in many groups due to casteism was also known to the British administrators which was the main barrier in the development of national sentiments.[1]

1. G.S. Ghurye, op. cit., pp. 175-176.

The efforts of non-acceptance of superiority of Brahmans have always been witnessed by history of India but non-Brahmin movement of this century is different from previous movements not only from extension and influence point of view but also from principle point of view. The lectures that the leaders of non-Brahmin movement delivered at Madras during 1920-1929 seemed to be influenced by European liberal and reformative ideas.[1] Non-Brahmin leaders laid emphasis upon the fact that they were equally superior as Brahmins were, and they wanted that British administrators might give them primary treatment so that they might be universally recognized as superior rank-holders.

Non-Brahmin movement was a response of depressed class of Hindu society to the challenges of castes of Indian peninsulas in new contexts of British regime and Western liberal reformatism. One of the founders of this movement was Jyoti Rao Phule (1827-1889) of Poona, by caste Mali who established 'Satya Shodhak Samaj' (the Society for the Search of Truth) in 1873 which aimed at propounding the significant importance of human being and humanity without considering caste factor. He urged non-Brahmins not to call Brahmins for ritual acts. In 1848, he, recognizing the necessity of educational expansion of non-Brahmins, founded a branch to educate non-Brahmin boys and girls. In 1851, he opened next branch at Poona to educate untouchables. He put his demand forth for the representation of all castes in services and local institutions.

There was dominance of Brahmins in administrative and simple services in whole Indian continent except Kerala state till the beginning of first world war. It was objected that Brahmins were favoured and non-Brahmins were discriminated and when non-Brahmins emerged as dominant, they harassed the Brahmans who worked under them. Prof. Ghurye[2] has

1. See the proceedings of the first provincial congress of the league of Non-Brahman Youth (Central) Madras and the administrative report of the league of Non-Brahman Youth, Madras, 1926-27.
2. G.S. Ghurye, op. cit., pp. 175, 183.

quoted a memorandum sent by Bombay government to the Indian Statutory Commission in 1928, by which it was learnt that in those schools of district board where non-Brahmans were in majority, they tried to expel Brahmin teachers without considering their academic efficiency.

Caste in Independent India

In no small measure due to the emergence of Western-style corporate caste bodies in both north and south India, the function of caste in Hindu society has radically altered in the last century, as many writers have endeavoured to show.[1] The Indian political arena today provides the setting for the most effective assertion of the interests of particular castes. It is also likely that caste interests and loyalties are the most influential factors in current Indian political life.[2] One half

1. e.g. M.N. Srinivas, "Caste in Modern India", *Journal of Asian Studies*, XVI, in which the author shows that strengthening of caste ties and the new functions, which castes perform are the result of British rule, in particular the expansion of communications and the development of a representative political system. See also F.G. Bailey, *Caste and the Economic Frontier*.
2. The new political importance of caste, operating within the limits of linguistically defined regions, has been unquestionably established in Selig Harrison's *India : The Most Dangerous Decades*. Harrison's conclusion might be tempered if read in conjunction with the ideas presented by Lloyd I. and Susan H. Rudolph in "The Political Role of India's Caste Associations", *Pacific Affairs*, XXXIII, I, esp. p. 9 : "The Caste Association brings political democracy to Indian villages through the familiar and accepted institution of caste. In the process, it is changing of caste. By creating conditions in which a caste's significance and power is (sic) beginning to depend on its numbers, rather than its ritual and social status, and by encouraging egalitarian aspirations among its members, the caste association is exerting a liberating influence . . . its successful assertions of privilege and rights are in many ways comparable to the extension of corporate feudal liberties which characterize the development of English liberalism. They are perhaps more truly indigenous assertions of liberties than the liberalism of the northern Indian middle classes."

century ago, however, most caste groups were directing their primary attention to improvements in their social and economic status; indeed, political questions were barred from consideration by the important caste conferences and sabhas. Many of the caste associations which were initially organized for non-political purposes later assumed political importance, while retaining their earlier interests in social and economic advancement. In independent India, the rate of intensity and activity of caste loyalty and casteism grew in the same proportion in which the Indian people began to get the political power and authority from India government. The transfer of power started from British period and ended till constitution of Indian republic, in which every adult was given the voting power in every five year election.

Bihar Congress displayed rampant caste based competition in 1951 election. There were three main castes—Rajput (which was led by the then finance and food minister Shri A.N. Singh), Bhumihar (which was led by the then Chief Minister Dr. Shri Krishna (Singh), and Kayastha (under the leadership of Shri K.B. Sahay, the then Revenue and Customs Minister). It was learnt through Times of India (3rd January 1952) that many congressmen were supporting many Nir-Dal contestants and frustrated congress leaders against authorised candidates. In short, Rajputs were supporting Rajputs, Bhumihars were supporting Bhumihars, and sometimes, denying the party-prestige and rules, Kayastha caste was divided into two factions out of which one faction was giving support to Shri A.N. Singh. Congressmen took the advantnge of theory of casteism.

Some reformative steps taken for depressed castes in 1951 were reported in a newspaper[1] which aimed at improving socio-economic conditions of low castes through establishing an organization entitled 'Shosit Sangh' in Uttar Pradesh. This is an indication of the fact that caste consciousness is increasing in U.P. It is possibly predicted that competition grows

1. *The Times of India*, November 14, 1951.

more between Rajputs and Chamars for winning political power. Rajputs lived in rural areas in separate groups till recently, but now, they seem to be more curious in awarding the status of Rajput to other aspirant groups, in order to strengthen themselves so that they may mobilize their political aim. Not only this, today every caste has become conscious of its caste-interests. Political leaders encourage casteism for their political victory and goal-satisfaction. The competition to avail socio-economic facilities is based on caste. Many educational institutions are established in the name of castes where the students of particular castes are admitted and given facilities. There are some other non-educational institutions where members of a particular caste are appointed. This results in frustration among other castes and caste-bitterness comes into being. There are many such temples which are established in the name of some particular caste members, they are run and represented by their managerial organization.

In 1947, when India realized independence, it was thought of abolising Zamindari system in order to improve farmer's condition. Gradually, this idea came into force in whole country. Ultimately, Zamindari system was abolished in whole U.P. on 10th January 1951 through an act. As a consequence of this step taken, some cases of robbery came into being in some parts of Uttar Pradesh, robbers were recruited from Thakur, Mallah and Gujar castes. Similarly, those Thakurs, Rajputs, and Gujars who were badly affected by Zamindari Abolition and Land Reforms Act of Uttar Pradesh began to rob in Middle India.[1] In 1952, these robbers frequently looted, fired and murdered untouchables of some villages of district Bhind and Muraina of Middle India. The editor of Times of India described that the movement started by ex-landlords against untouchable was a 'class-conflict.'[2]

In modern India, casteism and caste-tension are rooted in different steps and measures taken and used by India

1. Ibid., November 14, 1951.
2. *The Times of India*, January 26, 1953.

government. The policy of providing educational, economic, political and social privileges to the members of a particular caste may be equalitarianism, but latently, they have created cleavages and gulfs between higher and lower castes. Today, every one thinks that privileges should be given by government not on caste base but on economic base. Even privileged caste members internally agree with this view. A pilot survey of post-graduate students of a Post-graduate College at Akbarpur of Faizabad district was conducted and the conclusion drawn threw light on the fact that even scheduled caste privileged students expressed their opinion that government might give economic advantages to all those who deserve on the basis of their poor economic background.

Social inequality is curse for human society. Steps are being taken in this regard. Glen and Johnson[1] have quoted from unpublished thesis of Lelah Dushkin (1957), *The Policy of the Indian National Congress Towards the Depressed Classes —An Historical Study*, the different Indian Government programs for the welfare of Scheduled Castes and Scheduled Tribes—"probably nowhere in the world is so large a lower class minority granted so much favourable special treatment by the government as are the depressed class of India." The favourable treatment begins with the Constitution of India adopted in 1950. The Constitution abolished untouchability and forbids its practices in any form (Article 17). Article 15 (2) further provides that :

> No citizen shall, on grounds only of religion, race, caste, sex, place of birth or any of them, be subject to any disability, liability, restriction or condition with regard to—
>
> (a) access to shops, public restaurants, hotels and places of public entertainments; or
> (b) the use of wells, tanks, bathing ghats, roads, and places of public resort maintained wholly or partly

1. M. Glen and Sipra Bose Johnson, op. cit., pp. 69-71.

out of State funds or dedicated to the use of the general public.

In the Directive Principles of State Policy, a unique section stating the intentions of the polity but un-enforceable in the Court, the Constitution imposes upon the Government of India the positive obligation to assist the social educational and economic interests of backward classes (Article 46). The Constitution also contains several specific stipulations designed to aid the scheduled castes. Article 330 reserves 77 of the 521 seats in the Lok Sabha for scheduled caste persons.[1] Article 332 reserves seats in the State Legislative Assemblies for scheduled caste persons in proportion to their population in each state. Article 338 establishes the office of the Commissioner for Scheduled Castes and Scheduled Tribes with responsibility for over-seeing the progress of these social groups.

Parliament is specifically directed by the Constitution to implement Article 17 by making laws prescribing punishment for the enforcement of any disability arising out of 'untouchability'. In discharge of this directive, the Untouchability (Offences) Act of 1955 was adopted.

The Constitution provides provision of reservation of posts to appoint scheduled castes and scheduled tribes in Central and State Services. Under Article 35, having maintained the administrative capacity, the claims of members of scheduled castes and scheduled tribes are kept in mind at the time of appointments in central and state services. 12.5 per cent of seats are reserved for them even in open competitions held for filling up the posts in Central and All India Services. In recruitments other than above cited competitive recruitment, the reservation is raised upto 16.5 per cent. Instead, some states have shown best efforts to enhance betterment in economic, educational and social conditions of scheduled castes and

1. This provision was originally to last for ten years. It has been thrice extended for ten year periods and is now due to expire in 1990.

scheduled tribes. Some states have passed bill to provide special reservation to scheduled castes.[1] The bill involves different degree colleges and universities where some definite seats are reserved for them for admission in medical and engineering courses.

It is uncontroversial that caste system is most disturbing element in establishment of equality-based society, but by acceptance of some particular castes as backwards, the existing caste discrimination may remain continued, and it may also be that this discrimination shall prevail permanently. The strong and prejudiced sentiments of casteism today exhibit a naked dance in almost all spheres of human life. Today, untouchables realize a sense of legal security in its fullest sense and law and constitution are with them. They immediately react when a high caste person tries to depress or assault them. Sometimes, it is observed that they try to threat higher castes behind the curtain of law, and in doing so, they succeed even. Whenever dispute on a reason or issue takes place between untouchable and higher caste members, the member of untouchable caste immediately burns his hut and rushes towards nearest Police Station to lodge F.I.R. against higher castes. These cases are frequently obvious in rural areas of Uttar Pradesh.

Because of the certain legislative measures, provisions of social security to the untouchables, and grace shown by Gandhi towards them, they have shown a tendency of caste awakening, awareness and consciousness. They have also got their organized councils to meet, discuss and solve their grievances. A detailed discussion has been mentioned by Atal,[2] while studying the village Khiria which is located in the Sagar district of Madhya Pradesh. The district is an extension of Malwa Plateau. In the region of Khiria, the leather worker castes known by the generic term Chamar arranged a Sabha

1. Report of Seminar on "Casteism and removal of untouchability", 1955, pp. 98-100.

2. Yogesh Atal, *The Changing Frontiers of Caste*, op. cit., pp. 235-237.

(meeting) in Ron village in the year 1955. The pamphlet issued at that time is reproduced here. It began with a couplet.

> "Jisko Na Nij Gaurav Tatha Nij Jati Ka Abhiman Hai
> Vah Nar *Nahin*, Hai Pashu Nira Aur Mritak Saman Hai."

(One who is not proud of his honour and of his caste, is not a man; he is mere beast and like dead).

A translation of the pamphlet is given below:

Dear Charmkar (Raidas) Brethren,

By the grace of respected Bapu we are free, but social inequality still persists. This we have to eradicate by our good deeds so that we can progress and help the nation.

Today many problems face us. Our agriculturist brethren in the village do not accord us human treatment. We have difficulties in regard to cattle, labour, wells, tanks, etc.

The law made by the Government for our convenience is misused by the cultivators for their selfish interests. As a result, we poor labourers suffer in every way. If we make any kind of complaint, the responsible persons of the village prove it baseless and do not allow it to go further. Where there is a bidi industry, the cultivators close it down to compel us to work at reduced rates. If the poorer labourer does not go to his master without being called, he is troubled in many ways and as a result he takes refuge in the city and settles down there. Therefore, we request the village cultivators, clean caste Hindus (Savarnas), and the state government that, looking to our difficulties, they should treat us with kindness and sympathy as they did before and save the growing bitterness in the country and the deterioration of agriculture.

Our economic condition, the future of our children, should be directed towards the progress of our nation. If we were to obey the sermon of Gandhiji telling us to go back to the villages, we should be given facilities and opportunity to live in the villages. May our request not be seen with envy and may our interests be safeguarded in good faith. Our protectors (Rakshak) do not be our devourers (Bhakshak).

Raidas brethren are requested to contribute between Rs. 5 and Rs. 25 plus grain for the meeting that is to be held in Ron (Kumrai) to make it a success and to fulfil their duties. This pamphlet was issued by the District Raidas Committee and signed by 21 persons.

On another occasion in February, 1959, (when Shri Jagjiwan Ram, then Railway Minister in the Central Cabinet, visited Sagar) a backward classes Conference (Dalit Varg Sammelan) was organised. Pamphlets announcing the conference were distributed in all the villages. In this pamphlet the Railway Minister was referred to as Chaudhri, a designation used for the Chamar.

In the political area, and in socio-economic life, the lower castes have shown a tendency towards reinforcing solidarity. In other castes the trend has been in the opposite direction; the sphere and degree of control of caste councils, for example, have diminished considerably. There are instances where caste decisions have been flouted and recourse taken to courts of law. For example, a caste known as Kachhi Kudariya in Khiriya village took a decision against an individual who was keeping a woman who was already married to another man. This decision was not accepted by him, so the other party had to go to a court of law. Another caste Dangi of a neighbouring village started bidi-making, which was objected to by the caste members from other villages. The former, however, ignored the decision and continued bidi-making. Now there is no objection to their making of bidis.

There are many social factors that are responsible for bringing about changes in the various frontiers of caste.[1] One

1. Ibid., p. 243.

of the most important factors is migration, particularly to urban centres, with a view to permanently settling down there. Migration from one village to another within the same region, either temporary or permanent, is generally governed by (i) family reasons or by (ii) the purchase and/or sale of commodities etc. Moving permanently to a city is contemplated with a view to enhancing status by (i) change of occupation, and (ii) educational achievement.

Frequent visits to urban centres are greatly facilitated by the introduction of modern means of transportation. Visits to the migrated families bring new ideas of some slices of the urban pattern of living to the village. The families who have left show a change in dress and in occupation, and do not appear particular about the observance of traditional commensal restrictions. In urban setting and during travel the villager finds his position much less strictly defined than in the village; consequently, he finds himself relatively free from the norms that govern his behaviour in the village. Also a frequent visitor to the cities and towns gradually begins to adopt urban norms and to aspire for a life of urban amenities. Such people act as carriers of new ideas and innovations which penetrate into the village life. Such people are prone to occupational shifts.

A different factor, namely, the favourable and sympathetic attitude of the government in regard to the weaker sections—the untouchable castes—also deserves notice and mention. This factor has not only succeeded in abolishing untouchability but has rather had the opposite effect of motivating some revivalistic trends among these sections. It has helped strengthen the ties of caste. Caste consciousness has increased in the past few years. Srinivas aptly remarks in a newspaper article, "The tendency to continue to think in terms of backward and forward castes is producing new tensions and difficulties which may become more intractable in the near future. Actually many powerful castes have a vested interest in backwardness, and they will resist any attempt to remove them from the backward category." The higher castes resent or show anger towards the move of backward groups. In this context, it may be mentioned that the efforts at strengthening caste are being exerted at the level of caste clusters. The fact of a common name or the fact of backwardness is exploited in the formation of a caste-cluster based organisation. Such organisations are politically-oriented interest groups and do not, generally, aim at impinging on the endogamous frontiers of its sub-divisions. Where they do so, smaller sub-groups are merged to form a bigger unit with endogamous character and caste consciousness.

A case of caste-prejudice, caste-consciousness, casteism, caste-tension, caste-conflict and caste-war has been highlighted in a newspaper *Northern India Patrika* which reflects a high intensity and severity of caste-conflict between two backward castes Dhanuks and Yadavas in Piparia village of Bihar.[1] Caste-prejudices, so strong among the people of this area, have permented almost all facets of public life. The social fabric of the villages is woven around caste distinctions, and its economic structure demarcated by class divisions. Casteism is centuries old institution and governs traditional morality as well as an instrument of oppression. The big landlords of this area stroke the fires of economic and social discontent and prompt divisions in the ranks of the backward castes. The dynamics of inequality are inherent in this institution and the economic disparities have led to a polarisation in the caste structure conferring considerable social and political power of the landlords who use them to consolidate their advantages. They tend to monopolize government services and institutions and use them to consolidate their advantages. They tend to monopolize government services and institutions and use them to exploit the poor.

The village economy here is dominated by the Bhumiyars who own most of the land. But land is useless without labour. The Yadavas and Dhanuks, which form a substantial portion of the population, are mostly engaged in the fields

1. *Northern India Patrika*, 1984, Monday, January, 23, p. 3.

belonging to Bhumiyar community as agricultural labourers and share-croppers. A small segment of this section are marginal farmers forming the middle caste peasantry.

The landlord's influence and the power he wields extend the parameters of the village. With the wealth, he succeeds in buying the favour of the police, the judges and politicians. His gains are greater if the men in the administrative set-up are those sharing his caste sympathies. Perhaps nothing is as strong in the rural polity as caste solidarity.

It is in this backdrop that the series of killings that have taken place in Piparia and its neighbouring areas have to be viewed. The incidents are no isolated exhibitions of chivalry or bravado. Neither are they expressions of sudden emotional outbursts. The unending spate of killings is the consequence of decades of exploitations of the landless and middle peasantry. Frustrations are an offshoot of social staticism and progress is retarted by the scourge of caste politics. Agrarian reforms meet stiff resistance. Where class oppositions obvious—as between the labourers and land-owning caste—other social ties slice through them. The average villager is far more conscious of caste and tribe than he is of his economic class. The institutions of the law prevent equality before the law. The Yadavas of this reason earned the wrath of the power-wielding Bhumiyars with their entrance into the political process. This entry was facilitated by the breakdown of feudal relations in the rural economy. The top peasantry found themselves in a tight corner in which the middle castes had gained some economical strength following certain land-reform measures and the abolition of the Zamindari system. With economic power they started gaining political power. A rise in their strength evoked bitterness among the landlord castes. Antagonisms between the two castes began to grow and the battle lines were firmly drawn.

Cultivable land in this belt is scarce as the region is made up mostly of diara territory whose soul is not conducive for any agriculture and is covered with wild shrubs and Khas grass. About one-fifth of the area is annually submerged by the waters of Ganges and cultivation on such land is at best seasonal. Land hunger in this area, which has a population of about 10,000, had reached acute proportions in recent decades. The Ganges here is capricious and each year eats away large chunks of land, leaving their owners homeless and destitute. In other places they recede leaving silt banks of new fertile lands known as chars. Nearly a third of the Piparia region is char land which becomes the object of bitter and violent struggles for possession, invariably won by the richer castes, who can bring along the biggest contingent of armed relatives, supporters and thugs.

Many of the clashes between the Bhumiyars, Yadavas and Dhanuks in this region have revolved around the dispute of such char lands. There are strong indications that the recent kidnappings were a result of enmity between the Dhanuks and Yadavas over about 1500 acres of cultivable land.

In Piparia and its surrounding areas, there is no organisation of the poor and landless peasants who are hard put to reap the profits that may accrue from any agrarian reform. An attempt at building such an organisation had cost a 60 year old villager his life a few months ago. The poverty among lower castes is the greatest threat to their solidarity. Clashes frequently occur between the Dhanuks and Yadavas, which leave several dead on either camp. Such clashes are a result of competition with each other for the benefits—job or share crop land—that the rich increasingly control.

The administration is hard pressed to control the increasing crime in the region. The apparent failure of the police to arrest the criminals—only 20 per cent of the recent killings investigations yielded any arrests—had led to the loss of faith in the law enforcing agencies by the public. The local police strength is woefully inadequate and the ratio of the number of policemen to the population is perhaps the smallest in this region compared to the other areas of the state.

In modern rural India, due to advanced technology, mechanisation of agriculture, introduction of new scientific varieties of seeds, and use of chemicals in huger amount, lower caste persons have now begun to realize a sense of their economic advancement. Urbanization and industrialization have led them to tend to migrate towards urban and industrial centres. They are freely giving up their traditional occupations and trying to enjoy new and advantageous occupations, Some of them are being socialized through modern Western-oriented education and showing a change-oriented trend. Numerous of untouchables and low caste individuals in the country are becoming doctor, engineer, teacher, lawyer and clerk. Chitambar[1] has rightly pointed out that, "with the advanced technology, mechanization of agriculture, industrialization, and modern communication, disruption of the system and increasing conflict in traditional roles have occurred. Caste occupations and consequent roles are replaced by remuerative occupations, perhaps in nearby factories."

Chitambar further writes that "...the traditional caste system in India has in effect been disorganized through legislation, and while action on the basis of caste affiliation is illegal, the system is very much a part of the structure of rural society and the feelings of rural people."[2]

Social stratification may "set the stage" for inter-stratum rivalry and conflict.[3] Sich conflict may take various forms but in general results from an upthrust from lower strata to share equal rights with the upper strata and down thrust from upper strata to keep lower strata in their place. Such conflict frequently occurs when stratification systems are weakening,

1. J.B. Chitambar: *Introductory Rural Sociology*, John Wiley and Sons, New York, 1973, p. 83.
2. Ibid., p. 117.
3. Ibid., p. 233.

or in the process of disintegration being subjected to a variety of influential forces within society such as new ideologies, pressure groups, collective frustration of lower strata, and/or political and other interest groups. Examples of this phenomenon in operation are in the caste system in India, and in racial conflict in the U.S.A., South Africa, and countries newly independent or immediately prior to achievement of independence from colonialism.

I see, almost all villages of Akbarpur Tehsil of Faizabad district are disputed in one form or another. The population of all such villages is divided either in factions or in castes. Every faction or caste claims to be dominant. Similarly, every caste discooperates and looks down each other. Credit and obligation go to M.L.As. and M.Ps. in organizing lower castes against higher castes. These leaders encourage and provoke their castemen to pose their superiority and dominance thereby creating an environment favourable to recognize their influence at least within their own caste-communities. Sometimes, leaders from backward castes organize the whole backward castes against higher castes as a whole. This is also true in case of high caste leaders. It is reported that in situation of any problem, all castes utilize their leader's advice.

Numerous of examples of class conflict within caste system is contribution of modern era. There were mainly two issues involved in a conflict between Brahmans of Panjupur (Newada) and Bhars of Ashraf Patti (Newada) of Akbarpur Block. The first issue was related to the unnecessary dominance of Brahmans over Bhars and harassment; the second was related to the payment of lowest wage to the Bhars. Different sorts of harassments and assaults converted into physical coercion between the two. As a consequence, a Brahman was severely beaten and ultimately he was found to break his last. Likewise, in a village known as Rabipur Bahauddinpur, the main issue of conflict between Bhar and Kurmi castes was the village election of 1982. The election was fought by contestants on the basis of their castes. Due to casteism one of the contestants belonging to Bhar caste (Gaya Prasad by caste

Bhar) was declared elected because of having largest size of voters within his own caste community. The other issues are described in detail in fifth chapter.

The economic independence of and occupational mobility among lower caste persons have created a cleavage between higher and lower castes. This cleavage has resulted in caste tension. I remember an instance in this regard. Somewhat educated Chamar of Hariharpur village in Varanasi district of Uttar Pradesh used to respect the Brahmans when living in the village, but as he left the village for Bombay and got an appointment on a lower post in a hospital at Bombay and when he turned back to his village to pass some leave and holidays, this time a major change in his behaviour was observed and was found not doing 'pranam' to the Brahmans.

Although untouchability still persists in modern India as surveyed by All India Harijan Sevak Sangh [1] scheduled caste students experience frequent discrimination in University and College campuses, nevertheless, they have realized themselves as more protected and more secured. For example, in rural areas of Akbarpur in Faizabad district, Chamars experience themselves as more protected. In a village Hazipur Marui, there is tension between Chamar and Kurmi castes. The Kurmis of this area form a dominant group having more numerical strength, higher land holding, prosperous economic status and politically active. They do not have prestigious attitude towards higher castes. They are closely organized and form a close knit net. During Janata regime (1977-80) they emerged as power group and did every act right or wrong wilfully without any hesitation because their caste representatives were holding power position at state and national level. Although Janata regime went to extinction in 1980 and Cong. (I) came in power in the same year, but the mentality of backward castemen remained as usual. In Hazipur Marui, there is inter-caste tension between Kurmis and

1. *The Times of India*, 1983, Tuesday, March 29, p. 1.

Chamars over land issue. The land is under the possession of Chamars where they tie their cattles but Kurmis claim of their own. Against the super-imposition of superiority on the part of Kurmis,the Chamars face all the situation holding under the guidance of an young educated Chamar casteman who for all sorts of legal proceedings helps, supports and guides his men. The Chamars of this village do not afraid of any other caste as they consider themselves legally secured. They say, "Law is in our favour." By this it can be inferred that legal provision propounded by India government plays significant role in bringing confidence, boldness, enthusiasm and a sense of socio-economic and political security among the people of Chamar caste.

A somewhat similar situation is observable in village Dhir Ka Pura (Sijhauliya) of Akbarpur Tehsil where down-trodden community does not respect Brahmans. Due to educational enhancement among the members of such community, they openly oppose the deeds of Brahmans. They do not like to tolerate misconduct, misbehaviour and assaults done by Brahmins towards Harijans (Chamars). Tension is seen more acute when higher caste persons fail to pay the justified wage to working Chamars.

A case of social tension between Chamar and Brahman castes is also tangible in villages of Akbarpur known as Govindpur and Ganeshpur respectively. The most surprising phenomenon which has occurred in these villages is the awakening of Chamars under the direction and leadership of a Brahmin named as Shri Mahadeo Tewari. There is also intra-Brahmin conflict in these villages and the whole Brahmin community is divided into three groups each trying to dominate others through the exhibitions of possessions like wealth and agricultural facilities as teachers etc. No speaking term continues among them or it continuously in a least magnitude. Shri Mahadeo Tewari is also a leader of a group consisting of depressed castes like Rajbhar, Ahir, Chamar (some families), Mallah (Kewat) (33%) and carpenters. The issues of tension between Brahmins and Chamars is given below:

(a) Refusal by Brahmans to lay land left for scheduled caste people;

(b) To capture the same land by Brahmins in the name of religion, to construct temples or to use the land as play-ground and to prevent the Chamars to use the same.

From the facts cited above it is obvious that the Chamars face deprivation and frustration as their needs remained blocked by Brahmins.

India's stratificatory system which was based on cooperation of its constituent units in past seems to be marked by cleavages among different strata at present. Against the predominance of higher caste members, there has emerged revenging attitude among those who fall on bottom. The higher caste persons who had enjoyed a prestigious life, still want to enjoy the same by ruling over lower castes without caring the changed circumstances in modern age. In modern age, untouchables and backward castes are more organized than the higher one. In such changed situation, Brahmans and Rajbhars of village Panjupur and Ashraf Patti (Newada) of Akbarpur Tehsil have met conflicting situation over the prestige points and wage issues.

5

Analysis of Primary Data

In all 200 respondents belonging to different castes were interviewed with an interview schedule containing 72 questions in all, out of which 34 questions were common and rest 38 were divided in two parts. The first part containing question number 35 to 52 was meant for higher caste and the second part from 53 to 72 was meant for lower castes.

The organizational structure of different castes belonging to 4 villages studied has been identified and that is as under:

Table 5.1

Question No. 1—Opinion of the Respondents about their Informal Organization

Castes	*Class*		*Class*		*Total*
	Yes	*Percent*	*No*	*Percent*	
BR	12	32.43	25	67.56	37
KU	20	86.95	3	13.04	23
BH	105	99.05	1	0.94	106
CH	25	73.52	9	26.47	34
Total	162	—	38	—	200

In table cited above, the notations are as under:

BR—Brahman
KU—Kurmi
BH—Bhar
CH—Chamar

The table shows that Bhar caste members are mostly organized. Next comes Kurmi caste with a membership of 86.95%. The Chamar caste occupies the third place and Brahman the lowest. The data indicate that higher caste like Brahman is in the procsss of loosening its caste solidarity and backward castes like Kurmi and Bhar are showing a greater amount of caste solidarity and unity within themselves. The members of Chamar caste are also satisfactorily organized upto mark.

Some qualitative data on non-membership of different castes have also been generated in field situation and they respond that interpersonal jealousy of each other's individual possessions, differences of opinions, unwillingness to be organized, disputes on land issues, lack of affection, individual interests are the basic factors which have victimized some members of different castes and therefore they do not favour caste organization of their own.

Question No. 2: Table 5.2

The participation and the periodicity of attendance of the respondents in the meetings of their respective Caste Panchayats is noted in Table 5.2.

Out of total 200 respondents, 76.5% respondents attend the meetings of their respective caste organizations whenever meetings are held. Meetings are not held regularly but whenever they feel some sorts of difficulties they call on their respective castemen and hold the meetings. In meetings, different issues concerning their socio-economic and political lives are raised and put forth for discussion. Inter-caste relations are also discussed and misacts of opponent castes are

Table 5.2

Participation and Periodicity of Attendance

Castes	*Class*		*Class*		*Periodicity when meeting is held*	*Tota*
	Yes	*Percent-age*	*No*	*Percent-age*		
BR	8	21.62	29	78.37	When meeting is held	37
KU	20	86.95	3	13.04	,,	23
BH	100	94.33	6	5.66	,,	106
CH	25	73.52	9	26.47	,,	34
Total	153	—	47	—	—	200

seriously viewed specially in the meetings of backward and scheduled castes viz., Kurmis, Bhars and Chamars. The Brahman respondents do not show much serious trend in this regard as is evident through the table. Data on attendance of different caste respondents reveal that a least percentage (21.62%) of Brahman respondents show a tendency of attending the meetings of the Brahman caste. Majority of the Brahman respondents are aloof and do not take interest in the meetings held. This is the serious threat to Brahman caste community and if such situation continues, they shall loose their caste-unity, solidarity, strength and harmony, and thereby loosing their social identity, and thus, their social survival shall get endangered.

The attendance of Bhar respondents is highest (94.33%) in their caste meetings, then come Kurmi respondents with an attendance of 86.95% and Chamars occupy the third place. Brahmans come at last.

Question No. 3: Table 5.3

The subscription that the respondents subscribe to their caste organizations as well as to other organizations is shown in table drawn below. In most cases, it has been found that the respondents subscribe for 'Ram-Leela'. For caste organizations, the backward and scheduled castes subscribe when they are asked for. Brahmans, however, have no such provisions as they do not take interest nor create interest in the formation of their caste-organization. They are pessimistic in this regard. However, they subscribe for 'Ram-Leela' whenever they are asked for.

Table 5.3

Subscription for Caste/other Organization (Ram-Leela)

Castes	*Class*		*Class*		*Total*
	Yes	*Percentage*	*No*	*Percentage*	
BR	29	78.37	8	21.62	37
KU	22	95.65	1	4.34	23
BH	102	96.22	4	3.77	106
CH	26	76.47	8	23.52	34
Total	179	—	21	—	200

The data presented in Table 5.3 show that Bhar and Kurmi respondents tend to subscribe their caste organization and 'Ram-Leela' Samiti in huge number. The Brahmans here get third place (78.37%) and Chamars (76.47%) lie on bottom. The position of Brahmans higher than Chamar respondents does not mean that Brahmans favour their caste association but they figure more only because, they donate subscription to the 'Ram-Leela' Samiti. This donation has raised the number of Brahman respondents higher.

Question No. 4

The advantages that the respondents realize through their caste-organizations are shown in Table 5.4. The Brahman respondents being pessimistic in this regard are not too much hopeful with the organization. One thing that they bear in mind is that they have least amount of caste unity and therefore, the question of caste-organization does not arise. However, they are optimistic in the sense that if they get themselves organized they may be benefited by the way of their organization (Table 5.4).

Table 5.4

Benefit for the Membership of the Caste Organization

Castes	*Advantages*	*Class*		*Class*		*Total*
	A B C D E	*Yes*	*Percentage*	*No*	*Percentage*	
BR		33	89.19	4	10.81	37
KU		23	100.00	0.	0.00	23
BH		104	98.11	2	1.88	106
CH		34	100.00	0	0.00	34
Total		194	—	6	—	200

The data shown in Table 5.4 exhibit that equal percenage (100%) of the Kurmi and Chamar respondents feel that they shall get advantages by the way of their respective organization on different occasions. They say that they can get help in calamities, and in marriages. They express, the caste organization may promote the unity within the caste. It may also be supposed to be a device to develop a sense of co-operation among castemen. It may help achieve educational status and employment. The Bhar respondents expressing the same advantages by the way of their own organization show a percentage of 98.11, while Brahman respondents being optimist on one hand and pessimistic on the other, believe in such a conditional sentence that they can get advantages and satisfy their needs if they get their organization formed in the village.

Question No. 5

The respondents showing their patriotic attitude towards the decisions taken in meetings of their respective caste-panchayats have been classified according to their responses expressed in this regard. Table 5.5 represents such data and highlights the crux of caste-patriotism of different caste-respondents.

Table 5.5

Obedience of the Respondents towards Decisions

Caste	*Class*		*Class*		*No Organization*	*Class*	*Total*
	Yes	*Percentage*	*No*	*Percentage*		*Percentage*	
BR	8	21.62	4	10.81	25	67.57	37
KU	20	86.96	0	0.00	3	10.34	23
BH	104	98.11	1	0.94	1	0.94	106
CH	25	73.53	0	0.00	9	26.47	34
Total	157	—	5	—	38	—	200

The table shows that most of the Bhar caste respondents (98.11%) obey, accept and execute the decisions taken in their caste meetings. Next are Kurmi respondents with a percentage of 86.96%. Chamar caste respondents (73.53%) occupy the third place and Brahmans (21.62%) show a significant downward trend in this direction. The data also indicate that backward and scheduled castes in rural society today have not only their own caste-organization but they seriously support the organization in the interest of their respective castemen in order to safeguard their social positions in the villages. The Brahman respondents on the other hand favour to hold meetings of their castemen only when their common interests are involved and only in such cases they obey, accept, execute and implement the decisions. The respondents who answered in negative opine that they condemn the decisions taken in meetings if the decisions seem to be improper or wrong. This step is obvious in case of Brahman respondents. The Bhar respondents at this stage seem to be quite mum and a considerable highest frequency of their support to the decisions taken by their caste leaders indicate their blind faith not only in their leaders but also in their caste unity. They say, "Had we not been organized and united, the caste like Brahman and Kurmi would have eaten us." This was the response of a Bhar respondent named Afat of Rabipur Bahauddinpur village.

Question No. 6

Every caste, as is supposed, has a system of punishment for those who disobey and breach the caste rules. On such point, the respondents were asked to express their opinion about what really goes on with those who deny or refuse to accept the decisions taken in the meetings of their respective caste organizations. They, as per their observations as they felt, expressed in the following manner as is shown in table below.

Table 5.6

Non-compliance and Punishment

Castes	*Class*		*Class*		*No*	*Class*	*NR*	*C.*	*Total*
	A (Yes)	*Percentcge*	*No*	*Percent-age*	*Org.*	*Percent-age*		*%*	
BR	8	21.62	4	10.81	25	67.57	0	0	37
KU	20	86.95	0	0.00	3	13.04	0	0	23
BH	104	98.11	0	0.00	1	0.94	1	0	106
CH	25	73.52	0	0.00	9	26.47	0	0	34
Total	157	—	4	—	38	—	1	—	200

The table shows that majority of the Bhar respondents (98.11%) opine that in case any caste member fails to comply or refuses to accept the decisions, he is first of all requested not to do so but when it is felt that success is not possible, he is likely to be socially boycotted from the extreme of the caste majority and he is not permitted for any sort of social intercourse with the castemen. The castemen in such case do not like to interact with such man and he is prohibited at all stages in all manners. Talking term, food taking, water-pipe, marriage attendance, companionship, that all are stopped with such man. Next comes Kurmi caste with a percentage of 86.95% compliance and the Chamar respondents occupying a third place in the hierarchy of compliance of decisions taken in the caste-meetings and the Brahmans lie on bottom. However, in all cases and within each caste, there is the provision of social boycott and discontinuance of interaction including talking term, food-taking, marriage attendance, advice, companionship. These all are stopped with those who deny to accept the decisions of their respective caste-meetings. The table also reveals that there is a single Brahman caste which is not so rigid in penalising those who refuse to follow the decisions. 10.81% Brahman respondents witness this fact. The data higlighted in table show that there is no chance for Kurmis, Bhars and Chamars to escape from punishment in case they fail to accept the decisions. 0.94% respondent of Bhar caste gave no response on this matter.

Question No. 7

The opinions of the respondents about the punishment ought to be given in case a person refuses to comply the decisions taken in the meetings of caste organization (Table 5.7).

The data presented in table show that the majority of the Kurmi respondents (56.52%) are in favour of more punishment to those who refuse to accept the decisions taken in caste-meetings. Next come Bhar respondents with a percentage of 37.73%. The Brahman respondents (18.91%) show a more rigorous attitude towards the punishment than the Chamar respondents (14.70%). 17.64% of the Chamar

Table 5.7

Caste	*A*	*B*	*C*	*D*	*E*	*F*	*G*	*No Organization*	*Total*
BR	7 (18.91)	0 (0.0)	—	4 (10.81)	1 (2.7)	0 (0.0)	0 (0.0)	25 (67.57)	37
KU	13 (56.52)	0 (0.0)	—	3 (13.04)	7 (30.43)	0 (0.0)	0 (0.0)	0 (0.0)	23
BH	40 (37.73)	2 (1.88)	1 (0.94)	3 (2.84)	16 (15.09)	37 (34.90)	6 (5.66)	1 (0.94)	106
CH	5 (14.70)	6 (17.64)	16 (47.05)	0 (0.0)	0 (0.0)	7 (20.59)	0 (0.0)	0 (0.0)	34
Total	65	8	17	10	24	44	6	26	200

respondents show a liberal attitude in this regard and they opine that the disobedients ought to be given less punishment. Only two respondents of Bhar caste (1.88%) expressed their opinion in this way. 47.05% of Chamar caste respondents are of the opinion that the culprit ought to be given only that amount of punishment which is being given at present. Only one respondent (0.94%) of Bhar caste expressed his opinion in this concern. 10.81% of Brahman respondents are of the view that the culprit should not be given any sort of punishment. 13.04% of Kurmi respondents also think so, while Bhar respondents (2.84%) in least number opine in such a manner. The data on 'no punishment' indicate that Kurmis are more liberal than Brahmans while Bhars are very strict on the matter of punishment. 2.7% of Brahman respondents reveal that the disobedients ought to be given proper punishment. 30.43% of Kurmi respondents also think so and 15.09% of Bhar respondents support this opinion. The data in this regard reflect that the Kurmi respondents favour proper punishment more than Bhar and Brahman respondents while Chamar respondents are quite mum at this point. 34.90% of Bhar respondents favour the social punishment by the way of social boycott and stoppage of social interaction and disconnection of all sorts of social intercourse with the disobedients while only 20.59% Chamar respondents favour this sort of punishment. The other two castes are absent here. Keeping all the three castes aside, 5.66% of the Bhar respondents give more emphasis on casteman and they opine that the punishment ought to be decided by caste itself. This infers the united act of Bhar respondents who do not consider themselves as decision-maker but they wait for caste's decision and whatever the caste decides that shall be treated as final, they feel.

Question No. 8 and 9

For the identification of caste-leaders more influential in the views of respective castes and more influential and famous in the locality, the respondents were put to answer two questions mentioned at serial no. 8 and 9 in interview schedule, and their responses were tabulated in order to know the caste status of different leaders, the respondents consider as more influential and powerful. The data are shown in Table 5.8.

Table 5.8

Caste Status of the Leaders Identified by the Respondents in Locality

Castes	*Leaders*	*Caste Status*	*Yes*	*No*	*Total*
BR	1. Priya Darshi Jatli				
	2. Jiya Ram Shukla	BR	25 (67.57)	12 (32.43)	37
	3. Ramji Pandey				
KU	1. Jairam Verma	KU	23 (100.0)	0	23
	2. Hareram Verma				
BH	1. Chinta Ram Rajbhar	BH	76 (71.7)	30 (28.3)	106
CH	1. Swami Nath				
	2. Ram Pyare Suman (M.P. Cong. I)	CH	34 (100.0)	0	34
	3. Shri Ram				
	4. Babu Lal				
	Total	—	—	—	200

The table shows that the respondents do not segregate only on the basis of selection of their caste-leaders but they segregate in locality also while they consider the local leaders as more powerful and influential. The respondents perceive only those leaders more influential, powerful and problem solver who belong to their caste. The columns 2, 3 and 4 of first row in the table give a precise picture of the respondents' perception who prefer their caste leaders more important and influential not only within the caste boundary itself but beyond it also ranging from caste to locality. This infers that even today caste factor is considered to be crucial in the resolution of problems. That is, a high caste person in rural area perceives that only a high caste leader is the best and he can only solve the problems. On the other hand, a low caste thinks that only a low caste leader can give him shelter and solve his problem. This fact as observed in rural field situation is an indication and warning that caste system is not in the process of disintegration but it is re-enforcing in modern era. Casteism is rampant and is rooted in rural mind. The respondents who were interviewed and asked question no. 10 to 14, do not give the actual figure of men they meet, they contact and they are contacted by; the frequency of their visit to their caste households; and the number and the name of the other castemen who visit them; however, a general opinion of the respondents is recorded and they are described as under.

All the Brahman, Kurmi and Chamar respondents meet their castemen of their own locality not at a definite time and frequency but as and when they feel it necessary or randomly they meet by the way. This proportion is a bit less in case of Bhar respondents (99.05%) who also meet necessarily or randomly their castemen in the locality. The respondents belonging to rural setting and agricultural pursuit and continuous economic action do not have leisure to enjoy and therefore, the question of visiting the households of own castemen at a definite or regular periodicity does not arise. They can occasionally enjoy the companionship of own caste society or whenever they feel any sort of necessity, then only they do so. However, and whenever they get an opportunity to meet, they do talk and discuss on several matters concerning to the economic, social, political and cultural activities of their lives. Likewise, our respondents bear in mind not the exact figure of persons of their caste visiting their households but as and when the castemen feel any sort of necessity they visit the households of the respondents. The nature of their visit is not periodicial. It may be occasional, random or necessity-based.

All the respondents of Brahman, Kurmi and Chamar castes and 99.05% of Bhar caste respond that the castes other than the castes of respondents visit the households whenever they feel it necessary to visit not at a fixed interval but occasionally as and when needs arise. Similarly the respondents visit the households of their respective castemen not at a definite time period but according to needs. The respondents also do not visit the households of castes other than that of their own but as per needs. For example, a Brahman respondent may visit the working castes say Chamar, Bhar, Loniya for agricultural purposes. A Kurmi may visit Chamar, Loniya, Bhar and other agricultural labourers for working purposes. He may visit Lohar or Carpenter to repair his plough. He may visit Dhobi to get his clothes cleaned. Bhar and Chamar respondents may also visit Brahmans, Thakurs, Kurmis to render agricultural services to the high caste land owners. Thus, interaction between respondents and other caste members not belonging to the caste of respondents go on continuously on numerous of points specially on occasions where both the groups agree upon service-point. Low caste respondents viz., Bhar and Chamar who are supposed to be agricultural workers tend to render their services to high castes. On the other hand, high caste respondents interact with low caste persons when they tend to seek their services for agricultural as well as household purposes. By the elaboration of facts found in rural society concerning interaction among different castes it is obvious that 'Jajmani' relations still persist and rural people interact with each other on the basis of exchange of kinds and services. But it does not mean that there is warmth relation among different castes in rural society. Jajmani relations exist but inter-caste relations have also shown, on the other hand, a tensive trend today.

Question No. 15

The respondents were asked whether or not does competition between higher and lower castes exist. The responses of all the respondents have been shown in Table 5.9.

The data presented in table show that all the respondents belonging to Brahman, Kurmi and Bhar castes realize that

Table 5.9

Caste	*Yes*	*Class Percentage*	*No*	*Class Percentage*	*Total*
BR	37	100.0	0	0.0	37
KU	23	100.0	0	0.0	23
BH	106	100.0	0	0.0	106
CH	21	61.76	13	38.24	34
Total	187	—	13	—	200

there is competition between higher and lower castes. 61.76% of the Chamar respondents also think so. 38.24% of the Chamar respondents do not think of competition between higher and lower castes. The opinion of the respondents classified according to the villages they reside in, has been shown in Table 5.9 (a) which has been drawn below.

Table 5.9 (a)

Villages	*Yes*	*Class Percentage*	*No*	*Class Percentage*	*Total*
Ashrafpatti (Newada)	33	100.0	0	0.0	33
Hazipur (Marui)	36	73.47	13	26.53	49
Panjupur (Newada)	27	100.0	0	0.0	27
Rabipur Bahauddinpur	91	100.0	0	0.0	91
Total	187	—	13	—	200

The table shows that all the respondents of the villages marked on serials 1,3, and 4 observe competition between high and low castes while 73.47% of the respondents belonging to village Hazipur Marui feel so. Rest of the respondents of this village do not feel any competition between high and low castes. A comparison of Table 5.9s and 5.9(a) reflects the fact that the respondents who do not have a competitive trend between high and low castes are Chamars of Hazipur Marui. The two tables also indicate that almost all the villages under study show an emerging trend of competition between high and low castes which is an indication of rural dynamics instead rural statics. The rural people are now in the process of changing and the castes in villages are trying to compete each other as expressed by almost all the respondents belonging to different castes. A new pattern of inter-caste relations is emerging today and elements of competition are entering the womb of rural caste society, thereby substituting the elements of non-co-operation between high and low castes. The spheres of competition are many. Both high and low castes are trying to compete each other in all sectors of human activities, may be social, economic, political and cultural. The competition is more obvious in two villages which are Ashraf Patti (Newada) and Panjupur (Newada). These two villages which have given rise to inter-village, inter-caste conflict between Brahmans and Bhars are geographically very close to each other. In this case Brahman caste is considered as reference group for Bhars. The Bhars try to compete Brahmans in all respects. They think that their children should join schools and colleges to get education. They provoke their children to make career for modern jobs. When they come to know that Brahmans vote for Congress (I), they vote for Bhartiya Lok Dal.

They have also distinct cultural identity. For example, they have got their separate place to burn holi—a great festival of Hindu tradition. Cultural competition between Bhars and Brahmans is also manifest which radiates through the fact that when Brahmans arrange biraha (a folk song generally sung in little communities), Bhars also arrange the same and propagate that in such arrangements by Brahmans if 100 persons assemble, they would like the assemblage of 200 persons. Bhars have established their own Ram Leela ground—a symbol of religious Hindu faith and organize separate Ram Leela on the eve of Dashra (a Hindu religious fair concerning ceremony held on the eve of Victory of Lord Ram—the son of Dashrath—a King of Ayodhya in ancient India in the period unknown and controversial, and defeat as well as death of Ravana—the King of Lanka). Bhars tend to show a trend of imitation towards Brahmans while Brahmans do not tend to show such trend towards Bhars. This infers that when conflict takes place between higher and low castes, the degree of imitation in low caste is greater than that in high caste towards corresponding rival castes. By which it can be inferred that low caste has more competitive attitude towards high caste than vice versa. Brahmans do not take more interest in the activities of Bhars, however, they watch their activities not from competitive angle of vision but in the interest of their own safeguard. The two generalisations mentioned here hypothesize that conflict between high and low castes give rise to one way process of vertical imitation and competition working in low caste members towards high ones.

When two castes meet in a conflict situation, both form negative opinion towards each other. Brahmans consider Bhars as filthy, shirker, notorious, proletariat, and labourer while Bhars consider Brahmans as selfish, cunning, artificial, jealous, trickster, exploiter and dishonest.

Question No. 16

After knowing the magnitude of competition between high and low castes, the respondents were put to express their views about the impact of competition on attitude of their castemen to orient towards progress. Caste-wise responses of the respondents have been arranged in table in order to identify as to which caste is more progress-oriented. The quantified responses shown in table may be seen here at a glance.

Table 5.10

Opinion of the Respondents about the Progress due to Caste Competition

Castes	*A B C D E F*				
	Yes	*Class Percentage*	*No*	*Class Percentage*	*Total*
BR	37	100.00	0	0.0	37
KU	23	100.0	0	0.0	23
BH	102	96.23	4	3.77	106
CH	21	61.76	13	38.24	34
Total	183	—	17	—	200

The data shown in Table 5.10 drawn above obviously indicate that the competition between high and low castes has perfectly led Brahmans and Kurmis to develop feelings to go ahead. As is revealed by Brahmaṇ and Kurmi respondents, it is clearly understood that their corresponding castemen have now begun to realize that: (i) Hard work is essential to enhance economic status; (ii) High education should be achieved to compete the opponents; (iii) Power should be sought by the way of taking active part in politics; (iv) The youths should be sent outside to earn more money; (v) Commerce and business trade should be adopted and enjoyed; (vi) The castemen should be organized.

However, these feelings vary in Bhar and Chamar castes. 96.23% of Bhar respondents and 61.76% of Chamar respondents feel so. 3.77% of Bhar and 38.24% of Chamar respondents do not think the prevalence of such sentiments in their own castemen. Although the percentage of Chamar respondents who positively think on this point is lesser than that of the other three castes, but it is in fact a matter of surprise that they are too in the process of change and are struggling hard with their lives for their existence. It is an emerging trend towards change that Chamar respondents like to show through their shift from static stage to the stage of dynamics.

Question No. 17

In order to know the enhancement in the status of the castes which the respondents belong to, during last 10 years, the repondents answered in the following manner.

Table 5.11

Castes	*A B C D Yes*	*Class Percentage*	*No*	*Class Percentage*	*Total*
BR	35	94.59	2	5.40	37
KU	23	100.0	0	0.0	23
BH	104	98.11	2	1.88	106
CH	34	100.0	0	0.0	34
Total	196	—	4	—	200

In the light of above data presented in table drawn above,. it can be analysed that Kurmis and Chamars have been able to enhance their statuses in economic, social, political and cultural sphere upto mark as are reported by all the respondents belonging to Kurmi and Chamar castes. However, Bhar caste occupies a third position and Brahmans the last. Bhar castemen here top Brahmans by 3.52% which is the small margin. 5.40% of Brahman and 1.88% of Bhar respondents do not consider their castemen to be enhanced in socio-cultural, economic and political spheres.

Question No. 18

Voting behaviour of individuals in a society is a new social phenomenon specially in India who has become independent 37 years before. Since India has been declared as democratic, the power to individuals to vote for any of the contestants has been realized to be more in magnitude. Voting behaviour is shaped and determined by numerous of factors out of which caste is the most important. Whether or not do caste and politics go parallel to each other in rural society, the respondents were asked to express their observations about the bases of vote in the locality. Table 5.12 indicates the voting trend in the locality of the respondents.

An analysis of the table reflects a clear-cut picture of the voting behaviour of the persons in the rural areas of Akbarpur. The calculation of overall percentages, on the basis of total number of respondents, it becomes obvious that there is not a single factor in most of the cases which can be treated as determinant of voting behaviour of rural population. Out of 200 respondents 82 respondents (41%) reveal that the (voters) in the locality try to find out answer to three questions before going to polling station. These questions are:

(i) Which political party is more favourable and welfare-oriented for them?

(ii) What is the caste status of the contestant?

(iii) What are the attributes inherent in a contestant?

Only after getting well satisfactory answer to the above questions they encash their votes and deposit in ballot-box. 10% of total respondents say that people vote on the basis of political party to which they are affiliated. 12% say that people vote on the basis of caste and they favour their caste. 16.5% express that the people see both political and caste bases. 2.5% of the total respondents say that the rural people simply look at the quality of the contestants. 18% of the total 200 respondents report that rural people are unable to decide and they go on instructions given by the caste panchayat. Since the sample of 200 respondents consists of four different castes, different caste respondents observe voting pattern in the locality in different ways. In table, the opinion of different caste respondents has been shown and the percentage of their frequency distribution has been calculated on the basis of the total number in each caste category in order to compare

Table 5.12

Voting Trend in the Locality

Castes	*P*	*C*	*P+C*	*Quality*	*P+C+ Quality*	*Caste Decides*	*Total*
BR	10 27.02%	6 16.21%	18 48.64%	3 8.10%	0	0	37
KU	2 8.69%	1 4.34%	5 21.73%	0 0.0%	15 65.21%	0	23
BH	8 7.54%	17 16.03%	10 9.43%	2 1.88%	33 31.13%	36 33.96%	106
CH	0	0	0	0	34 100.0%	0	34
Total	20	24	33	5	82	36	200

the responses of different caste respondents. The table indicates that the political party base followed by persons in the locality experienced and expressed by Brahman respondents is greater than Kurmi respondents, is greater than Bhar respondents, is greater than Chamar respondents. 16.21% of Brahman respondents and 16.03% of Kurmi respondents feel that rural people vote on the basis of caste while only 4.34% of Bhar respondents feel so. Not a single Chamar respondent feels so in the locality. A comparatively greater percentage (48.64%) of Brahman respondents is of the opinion that the rural people follow a mixed base of polity and caste-statement is supported by only 21.73% and 9.43% of Kurmi and Chamar respondents respectively. Quality is also a base to vote for. 8.10% of the Brahman respondents think that in rural area, the people see the quality of contestants before voting for. 65.21%, 31.13% and 100% of Kurmi, Bhar and Chamar respondents respectively recommend the presence of three factors viz., political, caste, and quality as determinant of voting behaviour. The voters in the locality evaluate their contestants on the basis of these factors, then they decide as to what they ought to do. Looking at the last but one column of the table, it appears that only Bhar caste respondents (36 out of 106 i.e., 33.96%) feel that the voters wait for decisions taken by the people of the caste to which they belong.

Question No. 19 and 20

Casteism and inter-caste relations have been measured by asking a question, "Shall you disclose any fact known to you in court, if plaintiff belongs to higher or lower castes?" The responses of different caste respondents have been shown Table 5.13.

The data presented in Table 5.13 reveal that out of 200 respondents, 75 respondents (37.5%) agree to disclose in court only the true fact they know better in favour of any caste, may be higher or lower. Next are those who can simply disclose the facts in favour of their own castes. These figure (27.0%) out of 200 total. The respondents (17.5%) shall

Table 5.13

Opinion of Respondents on Disclosure of Facts they know

Castes	*A*		*B*		*True fact*	*In favour of Friend*	*In favour of None*	*In favour of own Caste*	*Total*
	Yes	*No*	*Yes*	*No*					
BR	13 35.13%	—	—	—	17 45.94%	1 2.70%	6 16.21%	—	37
KU	15 65.21%	—	—	—	6 26.08%	—	—	2 8.69%	23
BH	—	—	33 31.13%	—	42 39.62%	—	1 0.94%	30 28.30%	106
CH	—	—	—	—	10 29.41%	—	2 5.88%	22 64.70%	34
Total	28	—	33	—	75	1	9	54	200

favour low castes. 14% respondents shall favour higher castes. The respondents (4.5%) shall not like to go to court to disclose any fact. The respondent (0.5%) reported that he would favour his friend without considering his caste status.

Caste-wise description and analysis of table give another picture of the data. Out of Brahman respondents 35.13% respondents shall like to support a higher caste plaintiff. Out of Kurmi respondents, 65.21% of them shall also like to support a high caste category, but our Kurmi caste respondents who use their surname as 'Verma' are sanskritized and they perceive themselves as near to high caste members. This fact is clear when we come to know that a considerably high percentage (65.21%) of Kurmi respondents like to disclose any fact in court in favour of high caste plaintiff. Bhars and Chamars seem to disappear here from scene when the question of high caste arises. However, 31.13% of Bhar respondents shall like to go to court to favour low caste plaintiff. Casteism is more obvious in Kurmi, Bhar and Chamar respondents which lacks in Brahman respondents. 8.69% of Kurmi, 28.30% of Bhar and 64.70% of Chamar respondents opine that they shall speak only in favour of their corresponding caste plaintiff. Casteism, thus, seems to be more in magnitude in Chamar respondents, than in Bhar respondents. Kurmis have a very less amount of casteism while Brahmans carry zero-casteism.

Question No. 23

Table 5.14

Observation of Respondents about Inter-Caste Relations

Castes	*Yes*	*Class Percentage*	*No*	*Class Percentage*	*Normal*	*Class Percentage*	*Total*
BR	2	5.40	35	94.59	—	—	37
KU	3	13.04	5	21.73	15	65.21	23
BH	7	6.60	87	82.07	12	11.32	106
CH	7	20.58	27	79.41	—	—	34
Total	19	—	154	—	27	—	200

The data presented in table show that out of 37 Brahman respondents, 5.40% respondents feel that there is cordial relation among untouchables and backward castes today. 94.59% of the Brahman respondents hardly find warmth relation among different castes in villages today. Out of 23 Kurmi respondents, 13.04% respondents feel that there is cordial relationship among Ahir, Kurmi, Lohar, Barhai, Loniya, and Chamar castes. 65.21% of the respondents of the same caste feel normal relationship among all castes. 21.73% of the Kurmi respondents do not find good relations between any two castes. 6.60% of Bhar respondents observe that there is friendly relationship among Brahman, Kurmi and Kayastha castes. 11.32% of Bhar respondents feel normal relationship among Brahman, Kurmi and Bhar castes while a majority of the Bhar respondents (82.07%) hardly find good relations among different castes. Majority of the Bhar respondents feel that Brahmans and Kurmis try to make plots against them and hence the question of positive social relationship does not arise. A considerable smaller percentage of Chamar respondents (20.58%) realize that there is cordial relationship among Kurmi, Chamar, Loniya while a majority of Chamar respondents (79.41%) feel that there is tension among all castes today. The last row of the table indicates that out of 200 respondents 154 respondents (77%) feel that there is tensive relationship among all castes in villages today. Only 9.5% of the total respondents feel good relations. It is, therefore, confirmed that rural society today is characterized by inter-caste tension.

Question No. 24

The data shown in Table 5.15 throw light on the fact that all the Brahman respondents express that Bhar and Kurmi castes do not have positive relation with Brahman caste and, therefore, the social distance of Brahman caste from Kurmi and Bhar castes has become longer. 34.78% of Kurmi respondents feel that Brahman, Bhar and Chamar castes do not show cordial social relationship towards them. However, 65.21% of Kurmi respondents feel normal social relationship, 19.26%

Table 5.15

Respondents and their Relationship with other Castes

Castes	*Yes*	*Class Percentage*	*No*	*Class Percentage*	*Normal*	*Class Percentage*	*Total*
BR	—	—	37	100.0	—	—	37
KU	—	—	8	34.78	15	65.21	23
BH	13	12.26	81	76.41	12	11.32	106
CH	1	2.94	33	97.05	—	—	34
Total	14	—	159	—	27	—	200

of Bhar respondents feel that now-a-days there has become more friendly relationship between Bhar and other castes say Brahman, Kurmi and Kayastha, 11.32% of them find normal relationship. 2.94% of Chamar caste respondents feel more friendly relationship between Chamar and Kurmi castes. However, 97.05% of Chamar respondents feel negative social relationship between Chamar and Kurmi castes.

Question No. 25

The data presented in Table 5.16 indicate that 94.59% Brahman respondents feel that Bhar, Kurmi and Chamar behave like enemy with them. 5.40% of Brahman respondents do not consider foe-like behaviour of any caste with them. 34.78% of Kurmi respondents feel that Brahman, Thakur, Bhar and Chamar behave like enemy with them while a considerably larger portion of Kurmi does not think so. 41.50% of Bhar respondents feel that Brahmans, Kurmis and Kayasthas behave like enemy while more than half proportion of respondents of the same caste (58.49%) does not think so. Majority of Chamar respondents (79.41%) considers

Table 5.16

Misbehaviour of different Castes towards Respondents

Castes	*Yes*	*Class Percentage*	*No*	*Class Percentage*	*Total*
BR	35	94.59	2	5.40	37
KU	8	34.78	15	65.21	23
BH	44	41.50	62	58.49	106
CH	27	79.41	7	20.58	34
Total	114	—	86	—	200

Researcher taking an interview with a Brahman respondent of village Rabipur Bahauddinpur.

the behaviour of Kurmi caste full of enmity while a smaller portion of them (20.58%) do not think so.

Question No. 28

Table 5.17

Opinion and Experiences of the Respondents about their Stay at or Survival in the Village

Castes	*Yes*	*Class Percen-tage*	*No*	*Class Percen-tage*	*Total*
BR	22	59.45	15	40.54	37
KU	—	—	23	100.0	23
BH	40	37.73	66	62.26	106
CH	4	11.76	30	88.23	34
Total	66	—	134	—	200

The presentation of data in above table draws our attention towards the fact that approximately more than half of the Brahman respondents (59.45%) are afraid of opposite castes like Bhar and Kurmi for their stay at village. They are afraid of backward caste dominance. For example, a Brahman respondent named Kamala Prasad Pandey of Rabipur Bahauddinpur village reported his response like "I am living in village like Vibhishan in Lanka". The backward dominance in villages today have threatened the prestige and survival of some of Brahmans. 40.54% of Brahman respondents do not think such crisis now-a-days even. The social position of respondents seems to be quite safe and they feel not a single sort of difficulty in staying at village. They do not consider any caste so dominant so as to drive them out of village. Likewise, a larger percentage of Bhar (62.26%) and Chamar (88.23%) respondents shows that they too are enjoying a free and fearless style of life while a smaller percentage of Bhars (37.73%) and Chamars (11.76%) indicates that they suspect of their stay at or survive in village today. Over all, the social position of Brahmans in villages today seems to be weakest and that is deliberately being threatened, disturbed and hampered by low castes. Brahmans realize that there is lack of essential solidarity among themselves. The members of Brahman caste show outward sympathy and cooperation towards each other. They feel that Brahmans do not show very much sympathetic attitude and co-operative temperament towards their castemen. Also they are afraid that Kurmi, Bhar and Chamar castes are becoming organized against them to threat their prestige and influence.

Question No. 29

Table 5.18

Harm caused by Castes to the Respondents

Castes	*Yes*	*Class Percen-tage*	*No*	*Class Percen-tage*	*Total*
BR	33	89.19	4	10.8	37
KU	8	34.78	15	65.21	23
BH	43	40.56	63	59.43	106
CH	31	91.17	3	8.82	34
Total	115	—	85	—	200

The data shown in table drawn above exhibit that a considerably highest proportion of Brahman respondents (89.19%) feel a great harm caused by Bhars as Bhars have stopped working for Brahmans. 10.8% Brahman respondents do not think so. A smaller proportion of Kurmi respondents (34.78%) realize that they are being caused harm by Bhars. However, 65.21% of Kurmi respondents do not think so. 40.56% of Bhar respondents observe that they are being caused harm by Brahmans and Kurmis. The Bhars of

Ashrafpatti (Newada), Panjupur (Newada) and Bahauddinpur villages feel so. More than half of the Bhar respondents (59.43%) do not think so. In village Rabipur Bahauddinpur faction formation has created cleavage between Brahman and Bhars. Faction was formed over issues concerning village election for village presidentship. In Ashrafpatti (Newada) and Panjupur (Newada) villages, the issue was primarily concerned with wage payment to the Bhars which gave rise to numerous other issues and conflicts. 91.17% of Chamar respondents feel that they are being caused harm by Kurmis as is obvious in village Hazipur Marui. Previously, and now even, Kurmis have tried to suppress Chamars. Kurmis tried to capture land which was under the possession of Chamars (on patta) and on which the Chamars tied their cattles. Over this land dispute, tension between Kurmis and Chamars emerged. Chamars filed writ in lower court and ultimately they got success. Since then, Kurmis have begun to realize the identity of Chamar caste. Overtly relations between the two is seemingly realized to be a bit sweet, but covertly negative attitude towards each other continues. 8.82% respondents do not think that they are being caused harm by any caste in the village.

Question No. 30

Table 5.19

Response and Identification of Dominant Caste

Caste	*Yes*	*Class percentage*	*No*	*Class percentage*	*Total*
BR	6	16.21	31	83.78	37
KU	2	8.69	21	91.30	23
BH	40	37.73	66	62.26	106
CH	—	—	34	100.0	34
Total	48	—	152	—	200

On the basis of analysis of data presented in Table 5.19 drawn above, we come to know that 16.21% of Brahman respondents realize that backward castes namely Kurmis and Bhars are tending to become dominant in villages in recent time, and if they want they can drive them out of villages while a huge majority of Brahman respondents (83.78%) do not accept the dominance of any caste. Similarly, only a smallest proportion of Kurmi respondents (8.69%) have begun to realize the dominance of Brahmans, Bhars and Kayastha while a huge proportion of the Kurmi respondents

Researcher with a Kurmi respondent of village Hazipur Marui discussing on inter-caste relations in the village.

(91.30%) do not realize the dominance of any caste in the village. 37.73% of Bhar respondents feel the dominance of Brahmans, Kurmis and Kayastha while 62.26% of Bhar respondents do not feel any caste so dominant so as to drive them out of the village. There is not a single case of Chamar respondents who are afraid of any caste. 100% of Chamar respondents refuse to accept the dominance of any caste. The Bhars and Chamars because of having higher numerical strength in their corresponding villages do not realize the dominance of any caste. (Table 5.20)

Question No. 31

To trade out the sufficient unity and solidarity the respondents were requested to express their views. Their responses have been shown in table drawn below :

Table 5.20

Caste	*Yes*	*Class Percentage*	*Total Percentage*	*No*	*Class Percentage*	*Total Percentage*	*Total*
BR	9	24.32	4.5	28	75.67	14	37
KU	17	73.91	8.5	6	26.08	3	23
BH	104	98.11	5.3	2	1.88	1	106
CH	23	67.64	11.5	11	32.35	5.5	34
Total	153	—	76.5	47	—	23.5	200

The data shown in table exhibit that 24.32% of Brahman respondents feel that there is essential unity within the Brahman caste on the basis of common interest. 75.67% of Brahman respondents do not feel so because of differences of opinions, jealous, clash of interests, imposition of superiority upon others perception of high self-image, perception of self as highly intellectual. 73.91% of Kurmi respondents feel that their castemen are necessarily united. 26.08% of Kurmi caste do not feel a sense of unitedness within the Kurmi caste because of clash of interests, individuation, satisfaction of own interests only. 98.11% of Bhar respondents express that their castemen enjoy a high sense of unity and solidarity while only 1.88% of Bhar respondents do not think that their castemen are necessarily united. Bhars are so united because they have been considered and perceived by higher castes in the villages as weakest,poorest working caste. They have been depressed upto mark by higher castes, they feel. They now think that caste unity is the only way to survive in the village. They say that unity is the strength. They think, if they are not united, higher caste shall crush them. 67.64% of Chamar respondents express that their castemen are united. 32.35% of Chamar respondents do not feel their castemen so united.

In whole universe, however, 53% (total per cent) of (Bhar) respondents feel that their castemen are more united. 11.5% (Chamar) respondents feel that Chamar casteman are more united. 8.5% (Kurmi) respondents feel that Kurmi castemen are more united while 4.5% (Brahman) respondents feel that Brahman castemen are more united.

Question No. 32

Do you feel that some caste members are organizing against your castes ?

Table 5.21

Castes	*Yes*	*Class Percent-age*	*Total Percent-age*	*No*	*Class Percent-age*	*Total Percent-age*	*Total*
BR	33	89.19	16.5	4	10.81	2	37
KU	8	34.78	4	15	65.21	7.5	23
BH	95	89.62	47.5	11	10.37	5.5	106
CH	23	67.64	11.5	11	32.35	5.5	34
Total	159	—	79.5	41	—	20.5	200

The data placed in table show that 89.19% of Brahman respondents feel that Bhar, Kurmi, Chamar and other lower castes are organizing against Brahman caste to demoralize the Brahmans. Brahmans have been accustomed to exercise their influence upon the lower castes. They still want to continue the practice. In lieu of they expect of lower caste to regard them. But the time has passed and situations have changed. In modern age, every lower caste tries to enjoy freedoms in all walks of life. In trial, if it finds any sort of disruption on the part of other castes, it boils, and commits to give proper response. 10.81% of Brahman respondents do not find any caste organizing against their own caste. 34.78% of Kurmi respondents think that Brahmans, Thakurs and Bhars are organizing against their caste while majority of them (65.21%) do not think so. 89.62% of Bhar respondents consider that Brahmans, Kurmis, and Kayasthas are opponents, while a considerably smallest percentage (10.37%) of them do not considar any caste organizing against them. 67.6% of Chamar respondents express that Kurmis are organizing against them to depress and look them down. 32.35% of Chamar respondents do not express their views in this regard.

The data calculated in total per cent reveal that 47.5% respondents belonging to Bhar caste community feel the emergence of organizational front of Brahmans, Kurmis, and Kayasthas against them. 16.5% respondents belonging to Brahman caste community feel the organization of Bhars, Kurmis and Chamars against them. 11.5% respondents belonging to Chamar caste consider Kurmis as organizing against them while 4.0% respondents belonging to Kurmi caste community consider Brahmans, Thakurs and Bhars as their opponents. 2.0% Brahman, 7.5% Chamar respondents do not consider any caste as organizing against their respective castemen.

Question No. 33

On analysis of Table 5.22 it is obvious that 97.29% of Brahman respondents feel that lower castes, say, Bhars, Chamars, and other working castes do not co-operate

Table 5.22

Advantage of Weakness of Caste of Respondents taken by other Castes

Caste	*Yes*	*Class Percent-age*	*Total Percent-age*	*No*	*Class Percent-age*	*Total Percent-age*	*Total*
BR	36	97.29	28	1	2.70	0.5	37
KU	4	17.39	2	19	82.60	9.5	23
BH	51	48.11	25.5	55	51.88	27.5	106
CH	31	91.17	15.5	3	8.82	1.5	34
Total	122	—	61	78	—	39	200

the Brahmans. Brahmans being sufferer of disunity are ignored by the lower castes. Bhars and Chamars of the village do not like to go to them for agricultural and other sorts of domestic works. 2.70% of Brahman respondents do not feel so in the village. 17.39% of Kurmi respondents feel that Brahmans, Bhars and Chamars take the advantage of weakness of Kurmi caste. 82.60% of Kurmi respondents, however, do not think so. 48.11% of Bhar respondents opine that Brahmans and Kurmis take the advantage of weakness of Bhar caste. For example, when any scheme or facility is introduced by government through block concerned, Brahmans and Kurmis being clever and cunning use the same for their own purposes. 51.88% of Bhar respondents do not find such a case. 91.17% of Chamar respondents like Bhar respondents also observe that they are considered as weakest by Kurmis. Kurmis being dominant over Chamar try to enjoy the government facilities rather giving them to the Chamars. Kurmis utilize the facilities through the village Presidents who is also Kurmi by caste. 8.82—a considerably low percentage of Chamar respondents express that this is not so. The Bhar and Chamar respondents who answer in affirmative also reveal that Brahmans and Kurmis because of their dominance try intentionally to oppress the Bhars and Chamars.

Question No. 34

Table 5.23

Opinion of Respondents about the Possibility of Open Coercion

Caste	*Yes*	*Class Percentage*	*Total Percentage*	*No*	*Class Percentage*	*Total Percentage*	*Total*
BR	34	91.89	17	3	8.10	1.5	37
KU	5	21.73	2.5	18	78.26	9	23
BH	96	90.56	48	10	9.43	5	106
CH	25	73.52	12.5	9	26.47	4.5	34
Total	160	—	80	40	—	20	200

The data shown in table reveal that 91.89% of Brahman respondents think that they shall have to fight against lower castes specially against Bhars. 8.10% of Brahman respondents do not think so. The Brahmans are of the opinion that Bhars today have crossed the limit. They do not pay proper regard nor do they work for them. They are emerging today against Brahmans. They have threatened the prestige of Brahmans as is evident in Rabipur Bahauddinpur and Ashrafpatti (Newada) plus Panjupur (Newada) villages. 8.10% of Brahman respondents do not feel so. 21.73% of Kurmi respondents feel that they shall have to fight against Bhars and Chamars while a larger percentage (78.26%) of Kurmi respondents do not feel open coercion with any caste. 90.56% of Bhar respondents say that they do not like to touch and disturb any body but if they are disturbed and touched unnecessarily, they shall be bound to fight against Brahmans and Kurmis. The Bhars of Ashrafpatti (Newada) and Panjupur (Newada) say that they have already fought with Brahmans of Ashrafpatti (Newada) and if any situation conducive for coercion or direct fight occurs, they shall again fight for their protection. 9.43% of Bhar respondents do not opine such possibility in future.

73.52% Chamar respondents also indicate the possibility of physical or any other sort of coercion with Kurmis while approximately one-fourth of Chamar respondents (26.47%) do not now think of the coercion. They say that in a writ on land issue against Kurmis (of Hazipur Marui), they won and Kurmis got defeated. Since then, Kurmis have begun to realize the existence of Chamars.

Question No. 35

Table 5.24

Perception of higher Caste-Respondents towards Lower Castes

Response	*BR*	*Class Percentage*	*Total Percentage*	*KU*	*Class Percentage*	*Total Percentage*	*Total*
High	2	5.40	3.33	—	—	—	2
Low	35	94.59	58.33	23	100.0	38.33	58
Total	37	—	—	23	—	—	60

The data placed in table show that a smallest percentage (5.4%) of Brahman respondents feel that lower caste persons, say, Kurmis and Bhars respect them cordially while a considerably highest percentage (94.59%) of Brahman respondents do not feel that lower caste persons respect them cordially. The data also show that a lowest per cent of Brahman respondents have high perception towards lower castes while a highest percentage of Brahman respondents have low perception towards lower castes. Perception refers to the process whereby sensory stimulation is translated into organized experience. That experience or percept is the joint product of the stimulation and of the process itself.[1] An attitude can be defined as an enduring organization of motivational, emotional, percep-

1. Encyclopaedia Britannica, No. 14, p. 38.

tual and cognitive process, with respect to some aspects of the individual's world.[1] Here we may conclude that the perception of higher castes being lower towards lower castes gives rise to negative attitude of higher castes towards lower castes which ultimately leads to tension between higher and lower castes. All the Kurmi respondents also have negative attitude towards Bhars and Chamars. 100% of Kurmi respondents feel that Bhars and Chamars do not show cordial respect towards them. Majority of Kurmi respondents because of having lowest perception towards Bhars and Chamars have negative attitude which lead to inter-caste tension.

Question No. 36

Had the lower castes shown cordial respect towards higher castes, could they get the land ?

Table 5.25

Response	*BR*	*Class Percentage*	*Total Percentage*	*KU*	*Class Percentage*	*Total Percen. tage*	*Total*
Yes	6	16.21	10	1	4.34	1.66	7
No	31	83.78	51.66	22	95.65	36.66	53
Total	37	—	—	23	—	—	60

The data shown in table exhibit that only 16.21% of Brahman respondents agree in providing land facilities either for agricultural purposes on crop-share basis or for domestic purposes to lower castes. 83.78% of Brahman respondents do not express that they could provide lands to the lower castes. 4.34% of Kurmi respondents agree with the view that the lower castes because of their good behaviour and precise

1. D. Krech and R.S. Crutchfield, *Theory and Problems of Social Psychology*, McGraw Hill, New York, 1948, p. 152.

manner could get the lands for use or for agricultural purposes. However, a considerably highest percentage (95.65%) of Kurmi respondents are not in a favour of providing lands to the lower caste persons.

Question No. 37

Do the lower castes try to look down the higher castes ?

Table 5.26

Response	*BR*	*Class Percentage*	*Total Percentage*	*KU*	*Class Percentage*	*Total Percentage*	*Total*
Yes	36	97.29	60	17	73.91	28.33	53
No	1	2.70	1.66	6	26.08	10	7
Total	37	—	—	23	—	—	60

The data presented in table show that 97.29% of Brahman respondents realize that lower castes such as Kurmi, Bhar, Ahir and Chamar try to look down Brahman caste. 2.70% of Brahman respondents do not feel any lower caste looking Brahman caste and other higher castes down. 73.91% of Kurmi respondents feel that Bhar and Chamar castes look Kurmi caste down while a small and nearly one-fourth of Kurmi respondents (26.08%) do not feel that lower castes in the village look them down. In all 60% Brahman and 28.33% Kurmi respondents feel that lower castes viz., Bhar, Kurmi and Chamar look higher castes down. While 1.66% of Brahman and 10.0% Kurmi respondents do not think so.

An analysis of Table 5.26 (a) indicates that all the respondents (100%) lying in age group 15-25, 35-45, 65-75 and 75-85 feel that lower castes try to look down higher castes.

Table 5.26 (a)

Age (Years)	*Yes*	*Class Percentage*	*Total Percentage*	*No*	*Class Percentage*	*Total Percentage*	*Total*
15-25	3	100.0	5	—	—	—	3
25-35	14	87.5	23.33	2	12.5	3.33	16
35-45	8	100.0	13.33	—	—	—	8
45-55	6	66.66	10	3	33.33	5	9
55-65	11	84.61	18.33	2	15.38	3.33	13
65-75	6	100.0	10	—	—	—	6
75-85	5	100.0	8.33	—	—	—	5
Total	53	—	—	7	—	—	60

87.5% of respondents lying in age group 25-35, 84.61% of respondents lying in age group 55-65 and 66.66% of respondents lying in age group 45-55 feel that lower caste persons try to look down higher castes.

On looking at the column of total per cent of respondents, it is obviously clear that the respondents lying in age group 25-35 are highly frequented (23.33%) as compared to the respondents lying in other age groups. Hence, we can pass a concluding remark that the respondents in age group 25-35 have negative attitude towards lower castes which leads to caste tension between higher and lower castes.

The data presented in Table 5.26 (b) indicate that 75% illiterate respondents belonging to both Brahman and Kurmi caste category feel that lower castes try to look down higher castes. 25.0% of illiterate respondents of higher caste category do not feel so. 94.73% of respondents who are nominally educated feel that lower castes try to dominate and look down higher castes while 5.26% of nominally educated respondents do not feel so. 100% of highly educated higher caste respondents feel that lower castes try to look down higher castes.

Table 5.26 (b)

Education	*Yes*	*Class Percentage*	*Total Fercentage*	*No*	*Class Percentage*	*Total Percentage*	*Total*
Illiterate	15	75	25	5	25	8.33	20
Nominally Educated	36	94.73	60	2	5.26	3.33	38
Highly Educated	2	100.0	3.33	—	—	—	2
Toial	53	—	—	7	—	—	60

Out of 60 respondents, 60% respondents who are nominally educated feel that lower castes look down higher castes. 25% illiterate respondents feel so while only 3.33% highly educated respondents feel so. Hence, it is concluded that nominally educated higher caste respondents have negative attitude towards lower castes.

Conclusion

A comparison of Tables, 26, 26 (a) and 26 (b) highlights the facts that in comparison to Kurmi respondents, Brahman respondents have more negative attitude towards the lower castes. The Brahman respondents in a greater momentum feel a sense of dominance and tendency of looking down on the part of lower castes towards higher ones. Likewise, the respondents belonging to age group 25-35 have more hostile attitude towards lower castes and similarly, nominally educated higher caste respondents feel that today lower castes show a tendency of dominance towards higher castes.

Question No. 38

Whether or not do lower caste persons accompany higher castes ?

The data shown in Table 5.27 indicate that not a single Brahman respondent feels that lower castes accompany him.

Table 5.27

Response	*BR*	*Class Percentage*	*Total Percentage*	*KU*	*Class Percentage*	*Total Percentage*	*Total*
Yes	0	0.0	0.0	15	65.21	25	15
No	37	100.0	61.66	8	34.78	13.33	45
Total	37	—	—	23	—	—	60

100% of Brahman respondents feel that lower castes specially Bhar caste persons do not accompany higher castes. 65.21% of Kurmi respondents feel that lower caste respondents feel that lower castes such as carpenters (Barhais, Barbers, Dhobi and some members of Bhar and Chamar castes) accompany them while 34.78% of Kurmi respondents feel that lower castes specially Bhars and Chamars do not accompany but go on opposition to them. Kurmi respondents belonging to Hazipur Marui village opine that Chamars accompany them only on interest basis. At the moment, the vested interest becomes satisfied they tend to oppose Kurmi respondents.

The data in Table 5.27 (a) highlight the facts that equal number of respondents (25%) lying in age groups 25-35 and 35-45 feel that lower castes accompany higher castes. 33.33% of reepondents lying in age group 45-55 feel so. 38.35% of respondents in age group 55-65 feel so and 16.66% of respondents in age group 65-75 feel so. All the higher caste respondents (100%) in age group 15-25 feel that lower castes do not accompany higher castes Equal percent (75%) of respondents in age groups 25-35 and 35-45 also give an account of non-companionship of lower castes with higher ones. 66.66% of respondents in age group 45-55, 61.64% of respondents in age group 55-65, and 8.33% of respondents in age group 65-75 do not feel that lower caste persons accompany higher castes while 100% of respondents belonging to age group 75-85 feel

Table 5.27 (a)

Age (Years)	*Yes*	*Class Percentage*	*Total Percentage*	*No*	*Class Percentage*	*Total Percentage*	*Total*
15-25	0	0	0	3	100.0	5	3
25-35	4	25	6.66	12	75	20	16
35-45	2	25	3.33	6	75	10	8
45-55	3	33.33	5	6	66.66	10	9
55-65	5	38.45	8.33	8	61.54	13.33	13
65-75	1	16.66	1.66	5	83.33	8.33	6
75-85	0	0	0	5	100.0	8.33	5
Total	15	—	—	45	—	—	60

so. The data also reveal that the respondents (100%) lying in age groups 15-25 and 75-85 feel a strong sense of non-companionship of lower castes with higher castes.

The total or gross percentage of different age group respondents gives another picture of data. Out of 60 respondents, the highest percentage of respondents who have positive attitude towards lower castes and belong to age group 55-65, figure 8.33%. Similarly, the highest percentage (20%) of respondents who have negative attitude towards lower castes belong to age group 25-35 and they feel that lower castes oppose higher castes.

Conclusion

Brahmans have more hostile attitude than Kurmis towards lower caste.

The age graup 25-35 belonging to higher castes is most hostile group.

Hence, we may pass a concluding remark that higher caste persons belonging to age group 25-35 have more hostile attitude towards lower castes, say, Bhars and Chamars; and they feel that lower caste persons do not accompany them. This sort of feeling in higher castes but naturally leads to tension between higher and lower castes.

Question No. 39

Do the lower caste persons today want to live in co-operation with higher castes or with conflict ? (Table 5.28).

Table 5.28

Response	*BR*	*Class Percentage*	*Total Percentage*	*KU*	*Class Percentage*	*Total Percentage*	*Total*
Yes	0	0	0	12	52.17	20	12
No	37	100.0	61.66	11	47.82	18.33	48
Total	37	---	—	23	—	—	60

The data given in table show that all the Brahman respondents (100%) feel that lower castes such as Bhars, Kurmis and Chamars do not want to live in cooperation with higher castes but they want to create tension between the two. However, on this issue, 52.17% of Kurmi respondents answer in affirmative and they feel cooperation on part of lower caste viz. some members of Bhars and some of Chamars and others like Barhai, Nai, Dhobi, Kahar, Kohar, etc. 47.82% of Kurmi respondents express their negative attitude towards lower castes such as Bhars and Chamars. They say that Bhars and Chamars today have changed and they do not cooperate them. They simply cooperate on interest basis. [Table 5.28 (a)].

The data presented in table exhibit that not a single respondent in 15-25 age group has positive attitude towards lower castes. 100% of respondents in age group 15-25 feel that lower castes today want to live in conflict

Table 5.28 (a)

Age (years)	*Yes*	*Class Percentage*	*Total Percentage*	*No*	*Class Percentage*	*Total Percentage*	*Total*
15-25	0	0	0	3	100.0	5	3
25-35	4	25	6.66	12	75	20	16
35-45	1	12.5	1.66	7	87.5	11.66	8
45-55	3	33.33	5	6	66.66	10	9
55-65	4	30.76	6.66	9	69.23	15	13
65-75	0	0	0	6	100.0	10	6
75-85	0	0	0	5	100.0	8.33	5
Total	12	—	—	48	—	—	60

with higher castes. 25% of respondents in age group 25-35 feel that lower castes want to live in cooperation with higher castes while 75% of the same age group do not feel so. 12.5% of respondents in the age group 35-45 feel cooperation on part of lower castes while 87.5% of the same age group do not feel cooperation on part of lower castes. 33.33% of respondents drawn from age group 45-55 opine that lower castes want to live in cooperation and harmony, while 66.66% of the respondents belonging to same age group opine that lower castes do not want to live in cooperation but rather they live in conflict with higher ones. 30.76% of respondents drawn from age group 55-65 say that today lower castes want to maintain a sense cooperation between higher and lower castes while a considerably more than half (69.23%) of the respondents belonging to same age category do not feel harmony but rather a conflict situation on behalf of lower castes. Equal percentage (100%) of respondents belonging to age groups 65-75 and 75-85 say that lower caste persons do not show a trend of cooperation but they want to create a conflict situation.

Data calculated on totality of higher caste respondents give us a precise and more comparative picture of the respondents belonging to different age groups. A comparatively higher percentage (6.66%) of respondents belonging to age groups 25-35 and 55-65 reveal that lower caste respondents want to maintain cooperation and harmonic social relationship with higher caste persons while a comparatively higher percentage of respondents (20%) lying in age group 25-35 feel uneasiness and they say that lower castes do not want to create and maintain cooperation but rather they create conflict-situation. In table, as we proceed from 25-35, the data converted in total percentage (see column number 7) that show a downward trend except that on age group 55-65 with least total percentage on age group 15-25. By this, we pass a concluding remark that the respondents in age group 25-35 are most hostile. Next come the respondents in age group 55-65 while the respondents in other age categories show a tendency of lower hostility.

Conclusion

All of the Brahman respondents in comparison to Kurmi respondents observe that lower caste persons do not want to live in co-operation with higher castes, say, Brahmans and Kurmis. Therefore, the attitude of Brahman respondents is more negative towards lower castes than that of Kurmi respondents.

Most of the higher caste respondents who have negative attitude towards lower castes belong to age group 25-35.

Hence, we may pass a concluding remark that in comparison to Kurmi respondents, the Brahman respondents belonging to 25-35 age group carry a greater momentum of conflict towards lower castes.

Question No. 40

Is it true that the provision of eduction to lower castes shall make them disobedient to higher castes?

Researcher with a Brahman respondent of village Panjupur (Newada).

Table 5.29

Response	*BR*	*Class Percentage*	*Total Percentage*	*KU*	*Class Percentage*	*Total Percentage*	*Total*
Yes	19	51.35	31.66	18	78.26	30	37
No	18	48.64	30	5	21.73	8.33	23
Total	37	—	—	23	—	—	60

As is obvious from table placed above, 51.35% of Brahman respondents agree with the view that lower castes should not be given education otherwise they shall not obey higher castes nor do they work for them. 48.64% of Brahman respondents express their disagreement with this view. They say that education is an essential requirement of every citizen. It is positively correlated with rationality and intelligence. The low caste persons are fools. They must be imparted education. Only after getting proper education they shall understand the real situations and shall obey higher castes. This statement was boldly given by a Brahman respondent named Pandit Dharma Raj Shukla of Panjupur (Newada) village. 78.26% of Kurmi respondents disfavour the provision of education to lower castes while 21.73% of Kurmi respondents favour the provision of education to lower castes. 78.26% of Kurmi respondents agree with the view that the provision of education to lower castes shall make lower castes disobedient to higher castes. However, 21.73% of Kurmi respondents condemn such a negative view.

Conclusion

From the data in total per cent, we pass a concluding remark that the Brahman respondents in comparison to Kurmi respondents in carrying a greater momentum of negative attitude towards lower castes. They want to continue their prestige and practice the same on lower castes still today by the way of keeping lower castes illiterates. This behaviour as well as feeling of higher castes is surely responsible for the emergence of tension and conflict between higher and lower castes in rural society.

Table 5.29 (a)

Age (Years)	*Yes*	*Class Percentage*	*Total Percentage*	*No*	*Class Percentage*	*Total Percentage*	*Total*
15-25	3	100.0	5	0	0	0	3
25-35	12	75	20	4	25	6.66	16
35-45	5	62.5	1.33	3	37.5	5	8
45-55	4	44.44	6.66	5	55.55	8.33	9
55-65	9	69.23	15	4	30.76	6.66	13
65-75	3	50	5	3	50	5	6
75-85	1	20	1.66	4	80	6.66	5
Total	37			23			60

From table shown above, it is clear that 100% of respondents in age group 15-25 favour the statement that the provision of education to lower castes shall convert them into disobedients. 75% of respondents in the age group 25-35,

62.5% of respondents in the age group 35-45, 44.44% of respondents in the age group 45-55, 69.23% of respondents in the age group 55-65, 50% of respondents in the age group 65-75, and 20% of respondents in the age group 75-85 agree with the fact that the lower caste persons should not be given education otherwise they shall neither obey nor do they work for higher castes.

On gross level, however, the age group 25-35 shows a comparatively greatest percentage of respondents showing their disagreement on provision of education to lower castes.

Table 5.29 (b)

Education	*Yes*	*Class percentage*	*Total percentage*	*No*	*Class percentage*	*Total percentage*	*Total*
Illiterate	16	80	26.66	4	20	6.66	20
Nominally educated	21	55.26	35	17	44.73	28.33	38
Highly educated	0	0	0	2	100.0	3.33	2
Total	37			23			60

On analysis of table sketched above, it appears that 80% of illiterate respondents, 55.26% of nominally educated respondents, while non-percentage of highly educated respondents agree with the view that lower caste persons should not be given education otherwise they shall not obey higher castes. Among illiterates, a greater proportion agrees with this view. Among nominally educated, nearly half of them show their agreement, while not a single person among highly educated agrees with this view. 100% of highly educated respondents consider the provision of education to be essentially imparted to the lower castes. 20% of illiterates and 44.73% of nominally educated respondents favour the provision of education to the lower castes.

The total percentage of nominally educated respondents, however, is highest (35%) who agree with the view that the low caste persons should not be given education otherwise they shall not obey higher castes. Likewise, these are nominally educated respondents (28.33%) who feel that the lower castes should be educated. Here, we may conclude that the nominally educated respondents bifurcate on the basis of difference of opinion on this point. One group accepts and welcomes while other group refuses to accept the provision of education to be imparted to lower castes. But, since the percentage of refusers is greater than the accepters, it is confirmed that nominally educated respondents disfavour the provision of education to lower castes in order to maintain law and order in Hindu caste system.

Conclusion

Comparing the three tables on the same question, we conclude that nominally educated higher castes (specially Brahmans than Kurmis) belonging to age group 25-35 have more negative attitude towards lower castes and they disfavour their education.

Question No. 41

Are lower caste persons demanding more wage from higher castes?

Table 5.30

Response	*BR*	*Class percentage*	*Total percentage*	*KU*	*Class percentage*	*Total percentage*	*Total*
Yes	36	97.29	60	23	100.0	38.33	59
No	1	2.70	1.66	0	0	0	1
Total	37			23			60

The data at a glance show that 97.29% of Brahman respondents say that all the working castes such as Bhars, Chamars, Loniya, Jogi, etc. demand higher wage from land-owning higher castes. 2.70% of Brahman respondents do not have any such observation as they plough their fields themselves. 100% of Kurmi respondents validify the statement of the majority of the Brahman respondents on wage issue. They also realize a great labour crisis today. They say that labour problem is acute in village today. Whosoever are available, they demand higher wages. The land-owning higher castes are bound to pay them the demanded wage failing which tension, and sometimes conflict situation begin to prevail and show naked dance between higher land-owning and landless labour castes as is a case found between two villages known as Ashrafpatti (Newada) and Panjupur (Newada). The matter of conflict between Brahmans of Panjupur (Newada) and Bhars of Ashrafpatti (Newada) was concerned originally with wage issue. The Brahmans took more work from Bhars and paid only one ser (nearly one Kilogram) of superficial type of grain (Sava). Other issues then began to emerge around this and an admixture of which gave rise to conflict between the two and consequently a Brahman was murdered.

Data on total per cent indicate that Brahmans (60%) face a greater labour crisis and suffer from higher demand of wage than the Kurmi respondents (38.33%). By this, we infer that Brahmans have a bigger pocket of tension and conflict than the Kurmis.

Question No. 42

Is it true that the lower castes have been benefited by the land of higher castes?

The data show that 97.29% of Brahman and 100% of Kurmi respondents say that the lower castes such as Bhar and Chamar have been benefited by their lands while only one respondent (2.70%) belonging to Brahman caste does not think

Table 5.31

Response	*BR*	*Class percent-age*	*Total percent-age*	*KU*	*Class percent-age*	*Total percent-age*	*Total*
Yes	36	97.29	60	23	100.0	38.33	59
No	1	2.70	1.66	0	0	0	1
Total	37			23			60

so. Bhars and Chamars have been more benefited by the lands of Brahmans than that of Kurmis as expressed by 60% of Brahman respondents calculated on total or gross per cent level. 38.33% (total percentage) of Kurmi respondents feel that Bhars and Chamars have been benefited by their lands.

Question No. 43

Do you agree with this view that the lower castes shall not work properly unless they are beaten or abused?

Table 5.32

Response	*BR*	*Class percen-tage*	*Total percen-tage*	*KU*	*Class percen-tage*	*Total percen-tage*	*Total*
Yes	13	35.13	21.66	10	43.47	16.66	23
No	24	64.86	40	13	56.52	21.66	37
Total	37			23			60

On analysis of data presented in table sketched above, it is obvious that only 35.13% of Brahman respondents agree with the view that the lower castes who are meant for agricultural and domestic purposes should be beaten or abused. Then only, they shall work properly. These respondents believe in assaults of working castes while more than half (64.86%) of Brahman respondents read the time and situation and they say that now is not the time to beat or abuse lower castes.

However castes have now changed their socio-economic and political statuses and none can beat or abuse them. Also, there is legal provision for their safeguard. 43.47% of Kurmi respondents agree with this view that the lower castes should be beaten or abused in order to get proper work from them while 56.52% of Kurmi respondents disagree with this view. In total percentage, 21.66% of Brahman and 16.66% of Karmi respondents agree while 40% of Brahman and 21.66% of Kurmi respondents disagree with such a negative view to assault lower castes in order to get proper work. Here, the respondents seem to have liberal attitude towards lower castes not because they are liberal but because they are afraid of lower castes. Today, lower castes have also got a standing in the village because of their more numerical strength, economic independence and legal measures and provision for their safeguard.

In the light of above data, it is to pass a concluding remark that Brahmans are more hostile than Kurmis towards lower castes. [Table 5.32 (a)].

Table 5.32 (a)

Age (Years)	*Yes*	*Class percentage*	*Total percentage*	*No*	*Class percentage*	*Total percentage*	*Total*
15-25	3	100.0	5	0	0	0	3
25-35	8	50	13.33	8	50	13.33	16
35-45	4	50	6.66	4	50	6.66	8
45-55	2	22.22	3.33	7	77.77	11.66	9
55-65	4	30.76	6.66	9	69.23	15	13
65-75	2	33.33	3.33	4	66.66	6.66	6
75-85	0	0	0	5	100.0	8.33	5
Total	23			37			60

The data presented in table drawn above indicate that all the respondents belonging to age group 15-25, and equal percentage (50%) of respondents belonging to age group 25-35 and 35-45 reveal that they agree with the view that lower castes shall not work properly unless they are beaten or abused. 22.22%, 30.76% and 33.33% of respondents belonging to age groups 45-55, 55-65 and 65-75 also show their agreement with the view. However, not a single respondent lying in age group 75-85 agrees with such a view. Most of the respondents who condemn such type of view show a class percentage of 77.77% and they lie in age group 45-55. 69.23%, 66.66% and 100% of respondents belonging to age groups 55-65, 65-75 and 75-85 also condemn it. The data also reveal that the respondents (100%) lying in age group 75-85 are most liberal on this point. Next are the respondents lying in age groups 45-55, 55-65, 65-75, 25-35 or 35-45 show a downward trend on the scale of liberty. But it does not necessarily mean that these are most liberal towards lower castes. They are liberal only in the sense that they are quite aware of the facts that they are unable to beat or assault lower castes as the lower caste persons have today got the legal and social protections. The higher caste respondents find themselves incapable of fighting against legal and social protections being imparted to lower castes.

The total percentage of respondents gives us another picture of the situation. The table shows that a highest percentage of respondents (13.33%) lying in age group 25-35 represent the entire table who agree with the view that the lower castes should be assaulted so that they may work properly. Likewise, a highest percentage of respondents (15%) who disagree with this view lie in age group 55-65. Therefore, we can here pass this remark of conclusion that 25-35 is the most hostile and 75-85 is the least hostile age group. And, that 55-65 is the most liberal and 15-25 is the least liberal age group.

The data in Table 5.32 (b) throw light on the facts that 20% of illiterate and 50% of nominally educated respondents agree with this view that lower castes shall not work properly unless they are beaten or abused. 80% of illiterate and 50%

Table 5.32 (b)

Education	*Yes*	*Class percentage*	*Total percentage*	*No*	*Class percentage*	*Total percentage*	*Total*
Illiterate	4	20	6.66	16	80	26.66	20
Nominally educated	19	50	31.66	19	50	31.66	38
Highly educated	0	0	0	2	100.0	3.33	2
Total	23			37			60

of nominally educated and 100% of highly educated respondents disagree with this view.

The data (in total per cent), however, exhibit that nominally educated respondents who show a greater percentage (31.66% than illiterate and highly educated respondents (6.66% and 0.0% respectively), agree with the view to beat or abuse lower castes. On the other hand, these are the same nominally educated respondents who disagree with the view. Here, we find bifurcation among nominally educated respondents into two equal size of groups. One group supports the view while other refutes the view.

Question No. 44

Do you agree with the view that unless lower castes are threatened by court, the lives of higher castes shall be very difficult?

The data shown in Table 5.33 exhibit that 45.94% of Brahman respondents agree with this view. 54.05% of Brahman respondents disagree. 34.78% of Kurmi respondents agree and 65.21% of Kurmi respondents disagree with this view.

Table 5.33

Response	*BR*	*Class percen-tage*	*Total percen-tage*	*KU*	*Class percen-tage*	*Total percen-tage*	*Total*
Yes	17	45.94	28.33	8	34.78	13.33	25
No	20	54.05	33.33	15	65.21	25	35
Total	37			23			60

Data converted into total per cent reveal that 28.33% Brahman respondents in comparison to 13.33% Kurmi respondents carry more momentum of hostility towards lower castes such as Bhars and Chamars. On the other hand, 33.33% Brahman respondents in comparison to 25% of Kurmi respondents carry less momentum of hostility towards same castes. The higher castes who produce negative responses opine that lower caste persons can threat higher castes. They today knock at the door of court immediately. [Table 5.33 (a)].

The data presented in Table 5.33 (a) indicate that out of 60 respondents selected from both Brahman and Kurmi castes 10% respondents who agree with the view that unless lower castes are threatened by court, the lives of higher castes shall be very difficult belong to age group 25-35. Hence, 25-35 is the modal age group, the members of which show a greater hostile attitude towards lower castes. The respondents (3.33%) belonging to age group 75-85 show a lesser hostile attitude towards lower castes. The age group 25-35 seems to be liberal in the sense that a comparatively greater percentage (16.66%) of respondents do not believe in threatening the lower caste persons through court. Here, therefore, we pass a concluding remark that 25-35 age-group respondents bifurcate in two sub-groups. One sub-group (10%) supports the view while other sub-group (16.66%) condemns the view. Hence, 25-35 age group is not only hostile but liberal too on the point of provision of threat to lower castes by court.

Table 5.33 (a)

Age (Years)	*Yes*	*Class percentage*	*Total percentage*	*No*	*Class percentage*	*Total percentage*	*Total*
15-25	3	100.0	5	0	0	0	3
25-35	6	37.5	10	10	62.5	16.66	16
35-45	4	50	6.66	4	50	6.66	8
45-55	3	33.33	5	6	66.66	10	9
55-65	4	30.76	6.66	9	69.23	15	13
65-75	3	50	5	3	50	5	6
75-85	2	40	3.33	3	60	5	5
Total	25			35			60

From the analysis of Table 5.33 (b) it is obvious that 35% of illiterate respondents agree with the view that unless the lower castes are threatened by court, the lives of higher castes shall be very difficult, 65% of respondents belonging to same educational category disagree with this view. 47.36% of nominally educated respondents agree with this view while 52.63% of the same category disagree with such view. All the highly educated respondents (100%) disagree with this view.

Table 5.33 (b)

Education	*Yes*	*Class percentage*	*Total percentage*	*No*	*Class percentage*	*Total percentage*	*Total*
Illiterates	7	35	11.66	13	65	21.66	20
Nominally Educated	18	47.36	30	20	52.63	33.33	38
Highly Educated	0	0	0	2	100.0	3.33	2
Total	25			35			60

Out of 60 respondents 11.66% of illiterate respondents agree while 21.66% of the same category disagree with this view. 30% of nominally educated respondents agree and 33.33% of the same category disagree with this view. Only 3.33% of highly educated respondents show disagreement with such view. Hence, it is concluded that nominally educated respondents are more hostile and more liberal as compared to illiterate and highly educated respondents.

Question No. 45

Can the lower castes give up the works of higher castes wilfully?

Table 5.34

Response	*BR*	*Class percentage*	*Total percentage*	*KU*	*Class percentage*	*Total percentage*	*Total*
Yes	37	100.0	61.66	23	100.0	38.33	60
No	0	0	0	0	0	0	0
Total	37			23			60

All the Brahman and Kurmi respondents (each 100%) feel that all the working lower castes provide their physical services to higher castes in the interest of their own. Now-a-days, the working lower castes viz., Bhars, Chamars, Loniya, etc. have plenty of works to do anywhere, in any village or town. They are, now, not the bonded to higher castes. They are free to enjoy their works anywhere freely. The higher castes have no control over lower castes. Lower castes have become away from the grip of land owning higher castes. Higher castes cannot bind the working castes to work for them. Today is democracy. India is a democratic country. In democracy, every one has got some specific fundamental rights of freedom at least. Also, there are several government acts in favour of depressed and backward castes to provide them protection.

Question No. 46

If the wage to lower castes is raised, they shall be out of control. Do you agree with this view? (Table 5.35).

Table 5.35

Response	*BR*	*Class percentage*	*Total percentage*	*KU*	*Class percentage*	*Total percentage*	*Total*
Yes	31	83.78	51.66	8	34.78	13.33	39
No	6	16.21	10	15	65.21	25	21
Total	37			23			60

Out of 37 Brahman respondents, 83.78% respondents agree with this view that lower castes such as Bhars, Chamars, Loniyas, Jogis, etc. shall be out of control if their wage is raised. 16.21% of Brahman respondents, however, do not feel so. Out of 23 Kurmi respondents, 34.78% of them agree with this view while 65.21%—a considerably more than half—condemn this view and they favour the growth in wage rate of landless working lower castes viz., Bhar, Chamar, Loniya, Jogi and other castes of the same kind.

Out of total 60 respondents, however, a considerably higher percentage (51.66%) Brahman respondents as compared to 13.33% Kurmi respondents agree with this view. 10% Brahman and 25% Kurmi respondents do not consider any sort of disruption in social relationship between higher and lower castes. [Table 5.35 (a)].

From the data presented in Table 5.35 (a), it appears that out of 60 respondents, 18.33% respondents who belong to 25-35 age group agree with the view that if the wage of lower castes is raised they shall be out of control. Majority of the respondents fall in this category. Therefore, 25-35 is a modal hostile age group. However, 5%, 8.33%, 8.33%, 11.66%, 6.66% and

Table 5.35 (a)

Age (Years)	*Yes*	*Class percentage*	*Total percentage*	*No*	*Class percentage*	*Total percentage*	*Total*
15-25	3	100.0	5	0	0	0	3
25-35	11	68.75	18.33	5	31.25	8.33	16
35-45	5	62.5	8.33	3	37.5	5	8
45-55	5	55.55	8.33	4	44.44	6.66	9
55-65	7	53.84	11.66	6	46.15	10	13
65-75	4	66.66	6.66	2	33.33	3.33	6
75-85	4	80	6.66	1	20	1.66	5
Total	39			21			60

6.66% respondents belonging to age groups 15-25, 35-45, 45-55, 55-65, 65-75 and 75-85 respectively also agree with the view. The respondents shown in 'No' column of the table express that the lower working castes shall thus be controlled by the way of raise in their wage rate. 10% respondents belonging to age group 55-65 seem to favour lower castes more than the other respondents of different age groups.

Table 5.35 (b)

Education	*Yes*	*Class percentage*	*Total percentage*	*No*	*Class percentage*	*Total percentage*	*Total*
Illiterates	9	45	15	11	55	18.33	20
Nominally educated	29	76.31	48.33	9	23.68	15	38
Highly educated	1	50	1.66	1	50	1.66	2
Total	39			21			60

The data shown in table draw our attention towards the facts that out of 60 respondents, a comparatively more percentage (48.33%) of nominally educated respondents agree with the view that the lower castes such as Bhars, Chamars, Loniyas, Jogi, etc. shall become uncontrolled if their wage is raised. 15% illiterate and 1.66% highly educated respondents also support this view. While 18.33% illiterate, 15% nominally educated and 1.66% highly educated respondents refute such type of view. They say that by the way of raise in wage rate, the lower caste working group shall behave in a precise manner otherwise they shall show a deviant behaviour.

The higher caste respondents who express their views in affirmative are of the opinion that lower castes shall then demand more wage if their wage rate is raised.

Table 5.35 (c)

Family Type	*Yes*	*Class percentage*	*Total percentage*	*No*	*Class percentage*	*Total percentage*	*Total*
Nuclear	23	67.64	38.33	11	32.35	18.33	34
Joint	16	61.53	26.66	10	38.46	16.66	26
Total	39			21			60

The table shows that 67.64% of higher castes living in nuclear family agree with the view that the wage of lower castes should not be raised otherwise they shall be out of control. 32.35% of respondents living in the same family type do not feel so. 61.53% of respondents living in joint family feel that the wage of working lower castes should not be raised while 38.46% of respondents living in the same family type do not feel so.

The total percentage of the table show that in comparison to the respondents living in joint family (26.66%), the respondents (38.33%) living in nuclear family show their agreement on the point that the wage of working castes should not be raised otherwise they shall go out of control. This result indicates that a comparatively higher percentage of higher caste respondents living in nuclear family oppose the welfare of poor working lower castes. Their tendency is positively correlated with tension between higher and lower castes.

Conclusion

On the basis of Tables 35, 35 (a), 35 (b), and 35 (c) we may draw a conclusion that nominally educated higher caste persons (specially Brahmans than Kurmis) belonging to age group 25-35 and living in the nuclear family do not like to raise the wage of working lower castes. This unfavourable attitude of higher castes is positively correlated with tension between higher land-owning and working poor lower castes in the village.

Question No. 47

Do some castes obey you as usual?

Table 5.36

Response	*BR*	*Class percentage*	*Total percentage*	*KU*	*Class percentage*	*Total percentage*	*Total*
Yes	10	27.02	16.66	15	65.21	25	25
No	27	72.97	45	8	34.78	13.33	35
Total	37			23			60

From the analysis of table, it is clear that 27.02% (class per cent) Brahman respondents feel that some castes such as Thakurs, Kayasthas, Barhai, Dhobi, Nai obey them. 72.97% Brahman respondents opine that lower castes such as Bhars, Chamars disobey them. 65.21% Kurmi respondents feel that the castes such as Barhai, Lohar, Kohar, Kahar, Nai obey them while 34.78% Kurmi respondents feel that Bhars, Chamars disobey them.

Out of total 60 respondents, 16.66% Brahman and 25% Kurmi respondents feel that some castes (described above) obey them while 45% Brahman and1 3.33% Kurmi respondents feel that some castes viz., Bhar and Chamar disobey them.

Both Brahman and Kurmi respondents who answer in affirmative are of the opinion that lower castes are the friends of higher castes only because of vested interests. When the interests are satisfied, they do not think of higher castes (say, Brahmans and Kurmis).

The respondents, on the other hand, who answer in negative reveal the idea of social change. They feel that now a new era has emerged in which lower castes do not even care for higher castes, what to speak of obedience.

Question No. 48

If it is within their power, can the lower caste persons marry with higher castes?

Table 5.37

Response	*BR*	*Class percentage*	*Total percentage*	*KU*	*Class percentage*	*Total percentage*	*Total*
Yes	30	81.08	50	21	21.30	35	51
No	7	18.91	11.66	2	8.69	3.33	9
Total	37			23			60

From the data shown in above table, it is obviously clear that 81.08% of Brahman respondents feel that if it is within their power, the lower castes such as Bhar, Chamar, Ahir and Kurmi can marry with higher castes. 18.91% of Brahman respondents do not feel so about lower castes. 91.30 of Kurmi respondents also feel that lower castes such as Bhars and Chamars can marry with higher castes if it is within their power. However, a smaller percentage (8.69%) of Kurmi respondents do not feel so.

Out of total 60 respondents, 50% Brahmans and 35% Kurmi respondents feel that lower castes can marry with higher castes while 11.66% Brahman and 3.33% Kurmi respondents do not think so. The data here reveal that a considerably higher percentage of Brahman respondents as compared to Kurmi respondents have negative attitude towards lower castes which ultimately leads to inter-caste tension.

Table 5.37 (a)

Age (years)	*Yes*	*Class percentage*	*Total percentage*	*No*	*Class percentage*	*Total percentage*	*Total*
15-25	2	66.65	3.33	1	33.33	1.66	3
25-35	14	87.5	23.33	2	12.5	3.33	16
35-45	8	100.0	13.33	0	0	0	8
45-55	6	66.66	10	3	33.33	5	9
55-65	11	84.61	18.33	2	15.38	3.33	13
65-75	6	100.0	10	0	0	0	6
75-85	4	80	6.66	1	20	1.66	5
Total	51			9			60

The table shows that 66.66% of respondents belonging to age group 15-25, 87.5% of respondents in age group 25-35, 100% of respondents in age 35-45, 66.66% of respondents in age group 45-55, 84.61% of respondents in age group 55-65, 100% of respondents in age group 65-75, and 80% of respondents in age group 75-85 feel that lower castes, if it is within their power, can marry with higher castes.

The data converted in total percentage reveal that out of 60 respondents, a maximum percentage (23.33%) of respondents in age group 25-35 have negative attitude towards lower castes and they say that lower castes can marry with higher castes if it is within their power. In this sense, 25-35 is a modal age group which is a pocket of high tension individuals having negative opinion about lower castes. Next are those respondents (18.33%) who have negative opinion about lower castes lie in age group 55-65. Age group 35-45 with a total percentage of 13.33% occupies third rank on tension scale. The age groups 45-55 and 65-75 the 4-5th ranks, 75-85 age group the sixth and 15-25 the last rank.

The greatest total percentage of respondents, who do not believe that if it is within their power, the castes can establish marital relationship with higher castes, is 5% and these respondents belong to age group 45-55.

Conclusion

From the analysis of response on two variables caste and age, we come to know that this is Brahman caste in comparison to Kurmi, lying in age bracket 25-35 have more negative attitude towards lower castes (viz., Bhar, Chamar, etc.) and hence they are more hostile and lead inter-caste tension and conflict between higher and lower castes.

Question No. 49

Do you agree with the fact that the lower castes should not be given land otherwise they shall not work for higher castes ?

Table 5.38

Response	*BR*	*Class percentage*	*Total percentage*	*KU*	*Class percentage*	*Total percentage*	*Total*
Yes	27	72.97	45	23	100.0	38.33	50
No	10	27.02	16.66	0	0	0	10
Total	37			23			60

The table shows that 72.97% of Brahman respondents agree with this fact that lower castes who are supposed to be workers in the village such as Bhar, Chamar, Loniya etc. should not be given land in order to maintain the relation of production between higher and lower castes. A reasonably lower percentage (27.02) of Brahman respondents, however, do not think so. All the Kurmi respondents (100%), on the other hand, oppose the provision of land as gift to lower castes. The Brahman and Kurmi respondents who show their agreement on the question raised are of the opinion as to why shall a lower caste person work for higher castes if he is landlord ? Lower castes because of having least size or zero-size of land are bound to work in the fields of higher castes otherwise why shall they go to work at other places ?

The data shown in total percentage exhibit that the percentage of Brahman respondents (45%) as compared to that of Kurmis (38.33%) is greater and they oppose the provision of land to be given to working castes belonging to lower caste categories. Hence, it is concluded that Brahmans are more hostile and carry a greater momentum of tension towards lower castes.

Table 5.38 (a)

Age years	*Yes*	*Class percentage*	*Total percentage*	*No*	*Class percentage*	*Total percentage*	*Total*
15-25	3	100.0	5	0	0	0	3
15-35	13	81.25	21.66	3	18.75	5	16
35-45	6	75	10	2	25	3.33	8
45-55	8	88.88	13.33	1	11.11	1.66	9
55-65	12	92.30	20	1	7.69	1.66	13
65-76	4	66.66	6.66	2	33.33	3.33	6
75-85	4	80	6.66	1	20	1.66	5
Total	50			10			60

The table drawn above shows that the age group 25-35 of the respondents having a relatively highest total percentage

(21.66%) of all other age groups tend to show a negative response towards the provision of land to lower castes. Hence 25-35 is the modal age group having highest frequency of respondents who show a negative response towards lower castes say, Bhar, Chamar, Loniya, Jogi, etc. Next are those (20%) who belong to 55-65 age group.

Class percentage of the table, however, reveals that all the respondents lying in age group 15-25 do not support the 45-55, lower castes. In age groups 25-35, 35-45, 55-65, 65-75 and 75-85 there are respectively 81.25%, 75%, 88.88%, 92.30%, 66.66% and 80% of respondents who also refuse to support lower castes on the issue of land provision.

Question No. 50

Have the lower castes now begun to think?

Table 5.39

Response	*BR*	*Class percentage*	*Total percentage*	*KU*	*Class percentage*	*Total percentage*	*Total*
Yes	37	100.0	61.66	23	100.0	31.33	60
No	0	0	0	0	0	0	0
Total	37			23			60

All the respondents (100%) belonging to both Brahman and Kurmi castes observe that today working lower castes specially Bhars, Chamars, Loniyas, Jogis, etc. do not work honestly. They work wilfully and in absence of master, they begin to shirk. 61.66% (total percentage) respondents express their views in this regard. It may, thus, be concluded that greater percentage of Brahman respondents as compared to that of Kurmi respondents tends to show that lower caste persons are not faithful and loyal to their master. They do not care for the loss of employing higher caste land owners.

Nor do they consider the work of their employer—higher caste as the work of their own. They have 'They' feeling instead of 'we' feeling which threatens the village unity and inter-caste relations become tense.

Question No. 51

Are the lower caste persons disobeying now?

Table 5.40

Response	*BR*	*Class percentage*	*Total percentage*	*KU*	*Class percentage*	*Total percentage*	*Total*
Yes	22	59.45	36.66	23	100.0	38.33	45
No	0	0	0	0	0	0	0
A	15	40.54	25	0	0	0	15
Total	37			23			60

The data shown in table drawn above indicate that 59.45% of Brahman respondents feel that lower castes such as Bhar, Chamar, Ahir, Kurmi etc. disobey them. However, 40.54% of the respondents belonging to same caste opine that lower castes simply obey them when they feel some problems or when they need something from higher castes. Otherwise, after the satisfaction of needs or solution of problems, they ignore and avoid the higher castes. 100% Kurmi respondents opine that Bhar and Chamar castes interact with them due to vested interest. After the interests being satisfied they do not obey nor do they pay proper regard to them.

Question No. 52

Are the lower caste persons trying to threat the prestige of higher caste persons ?

On analysis of Table 5.41 it appears that 97.29% of Brahman respondents feel that lower castes such as Bhar, Chamar, Ahir,

Table 5.41

Response	*BR*	*Class percentage*	*Total percentage*	*KU*	*Class percentage*	*Total percentage*	*Total*
Yes	36	97.29	60	23	100.0	38.33	59
No	1	2.70	1.66	0	0	0	1
Total	37			23			60

Kurmi show a negative attitude towards Brahmans and other higher castes. They have now begun to ignore, avoid and disobey their super-castes. They have now changed and do not give proper regard nor do they pay attention to the higher castes. 2.70% of Brahman respondents, however, do not feel so. 100% of Kurmi respondents also have an observation of the behaviour of lower castes viz., Bhar and Chamar who try to disrupt the ritual caste hierarchy and do not consider themselves less than higher castes.

Table 5.41 (a)

Age (years)	*Yes*	*Class percentage*	*Total percentage*	*No*	*Class percentage*	*Total percentage*	*Total*
15-25	3	100.0	5	0	0	0	3
25-35	16	100.0	26.66	0	0	0	16
35-45	8	100.00	13.33	0	0	0	8
45-55	9	100.0	15	0	0	0	9
55-65	12	92.30	20	1	7.69	1.66	13
65-75	6	100.0	10	0	0	0	6
75-85	5	100.0	8.33	0	0	0	5
Total	59			1			60

The data shown in table indicate a surprising picture of respondents who give their opinion, observation and experience about their prestige which is being threatened by lower castes.

Equal percentage (class percentage) of respondents (100%) equally belonging to different age groups except the age group 55-65 who are anxious of their prestige which is in danger today in villages as the lower castes such as Bhar, Chamar, Ahir etc. have left them to recognize as more prestigious and influential today. The democratic pattern of village franchise has created a new avenue of dynamics of power and the lower castes have now begun to enjoy the same as is a case in Rabipur Bahauddinpur village where a Bhar, known as Gaya Prasad is the chief of the village.

Likewise, the Chamars of village Hazipur Marui nominate their own casteman as contestant against Kurmi candidate. A faction situation as well as inter-caste tension between Kurmis and Chamars of this village seems to be frequently apparent in every village-election. Similarly, the factionalism and tension situation among different castes of the village Rabipur Bahauddinpur are the consequences of village-election. The Kurmi candidate of this village could not get elected in previous election even after the support of Brahman while the Bhar candidate because of having more voters within the Bhar community was declared elected. This political base of inter-caste tension gave later on rise to numerous of conflicts and whole village even today has become an arena of conflict. 92.30% of respondents belonging to age group 55-65 feel that lower castes are threatening their social prestige.

On looking at the total percentage of the table, the picture of situation is more apparent and it is the age group 25-35 which is most frequented (26.66%) in comparison to other age groups.

It is apparent from Table 5.41 (b) that 100% of illiterate, 97.36% of nominally educated, and 100% of highly educated respondents feel that their social prestige is in danger. 2.63% of nominally educated respondents do not think so.

Table 5.41 (b)

Education	*Yes*	*Class percentage*	*Total percentage*	*No*	*Class percentage*	*Total percentage*	*Total*
Illiterates	20	100.0	33.33	0	0	0	20
Nominally Educated	37	97.36	61.66	1	2.63	1.66	38
Highly Educated	2	100.0	3.33	0	0	0	2
Total	59			1			60

The total percentage of the table precisely indicate that a relatively highest percentage (61.66%) of nominally educated respondents feel that lower castes such as Bhars, Chamars, Ahirs etc. are trying to hamper their social prestige. 33.33% of illiterate respondents and 3.33% of highly educated respondents also feel so while 1.66% of nominally educated respondents which is negligible in number do not feel such prestige-crisis.

Table 5.41 (c)

Family Type	*Yes*	*Class percentage*	*Total percentage*	*No*	*Class percentage*	*Total percentage*	*Total*
Nuclear	34	100.0	56.66	0	0	0	34
Joint	25	96.15	41.66	1	3.84	1.66	26
Total	59			1			60

The table shows that all the higher caste respondents in nuclear family feel that lower caste persons are trying to threat their prestige. 96.15% of higher caste respondents in joint family have also formed the same opinion while 3.84% of respondents do not find their prestige in danger.

The total percentage of data indicate that in comparison to the respondents living in joint fumily (41.66%), the respondents living in nuclear family (56.66%) feel a greater prestige-crisis and hence, they have got a greater tension-pocket towards lower caste persons, say, Bhars and Chamars, Ahirs and Kurmis etc. Hence, it is concluded that in villages today it is nuclear family rather joint one which leads to caste-tension and conflict between higher and lower castes.

Conclusion

On the basis of analysis of Tables 5.41, 5.41(a), 5.41(b) and 5.41 (c), we pass a conclusion of remark that nominally educated higher caste persons specially Brahmans than Kurmis lying in age group 25-35 and belonging to nuclear family are responsible for the emergence of inter-caste conflict apparent on village scene today.

Question No. 53

Perception of lower caste respondents about higher castes.

Table 5.42

Response	*BH*	*Class percen-tage*	*Total percen-tage*	*CH*	*Class percen-tage*	*Total percen-tage*	*Total*
High	11	10.37	7.85	9	26.47	6.42	20
Low	95	89.62	67.85	25	73.52	17.85	120
Total	106			34			140

The data presented in table show that only 10.37% of Brahman respondents have high perception towards higher castes such as Brahmans, Kurmis, Kayastha, Thakur, etc. Majority of Bhar respondents (89.62%) has a generally low perception towards Brahmans, Kurmis, Kayasthas,

Thakurs, etc. On the other hand, 26.47% of Chamar respondents have high perception towards higher castes, say, Brahmans and Kurmis; but a considerably higher percentage (73.52%) of Chamar respondents have low perception and low impression towards higher castes.

The data in total percent reveal that Bhars (7.85%) have higher perception towards higher castes as compared to that of Chamars (6.42%). Similarly Bhars (67.85) have lower perception towards higher castes as compared to that of Chamar respondents (17.85%).

Perception and attitude are positively correlated. An individual who perceives other individual as friend has a positive attitude towards that individual and behaves friendly. Otherwise vice-versa. That is, higher the perception, more positive shall be the attitude and consequently more the social interaction and more the friendly relation. Lower the perception, more negative the attitude and consequently lesser the social interaction and more the tension in social relationship between percepter and the percepted object.

Bhars and Chamars in greater percentage have lower perception towards higher castes. They have sufficiently negative attitude towards them which ultimately leads to negative social relationship between higher and lower castes. The majority of Bhars and Chamars feel that the higher castes like Brahman, Thakur, Kurmi do not love or respect them by heart.

Table 5.43

Response	*BH*	*Class percentage*	*Total percentage*	*CH*	*Class percentage*	*Total percentage*	*Total*
Yes	21	19.81	15	3	8.82	2.14	24
No	85	80.18	60.71	31	91.17	22.14	116
Total	106			34			140

Question No. 54

Had the higher castes done so, could they have got the lands of lower castes?

The data show that 19.81% of Bhars and 8.82% of Chamar respondents express that any person because of his virtue of cordial love, affection, respect, etiquette, precise manner, character may get lands for-any sort of use. However, the majority of Bhar (80.18%) and Chamar (91.17%) express that they have acute shortage of lands. Therefore, the question of providing lands to higher castes does not arise.

The data in total percentage indicate that 15% Bhar respondents as compared to the 2.14% Chamar respondent agree to provide lands to higher castes while 60.71% of Bhar respondents as compared to 22.14% of Chamar respondents are not in a position to provide land to higher castes like Brahmans, Kurmis, etc.

Question No. 55

Are the higher caste persons trying to dominate/look down lower castes ?

Table 5.44

Response	*BH*	*Class percentage*	*Total percentage*	*CH*	*Class percentage*	*Total percentage*	*Total*
Yes	99	93.39	70.71	30	88.23	21.42	129
No	7	6.60	5	4	11.76	2.85	11
Total	106			34			140

The data shown in table reflect the fact that 93.39% of Bhar respondents feel that higher castes like Brahman, Kurmi are trying to dominate them. In previous village-election for the presidentship, the Brahmans and Kurmis of Rabipur Bahauddinpur village jointly tried to defeat the candidate of Bhar caste. But Bhar candidate because of having a comparatively higher number of voters was declared won. Brahmans and Kurmis were organized against Bhars and started non-cooperation movement against them such as refusal to give water of their own pump-sets for irrigation. Bhars of Panjupur (Newada) and Ashrafpatti (Newada) were also opposed by Brahmans of Panjupur (Newada) on wage issue and other related matters. They were disallowed to enter the Brahman's fields. They were commented by Brahmans. They were prohibited to attend the public meetings of leaders. In case some members of Bhar caste tried to go there, they were passed remarks of being leader by Brahmans. They were prohibited and checked to pass by the gate or land of Brahmans. They were assaulted when their cattles went into the Brahman's field. These were all with Bhars on the part of Brahmans. 6.60% of Bhar respondents do not feel so. 88.23% of Chamar respondents observe that all the higher castes viz., Brahman, Thakur, Kurmi try to dominate or look them down. Chamars of Hazipur Marui village were always disturbed by Kurmis. Kurmis considered Chamars as weakest. Over the issue of a land which the Chamars had taken on lease and where they tied their cattles to take rest, the Kurmis tried to capture. Dispute took place between the two castes. Chamars filed law-suit in lower court of Faizabad and decision went in their favour. Since then Kurmis have begun to show a change in their behaviour and have begun to interact with Chamars frequently. Overt conflict in this village does not seem to be apparent but it does not mean that conflict between the two does not prevail. It prevails but convertly. 11.76% of Chamar respondents feel that conflict situation has now become normalized and Kurmis of the village do not try to dominate them because of their glorious victory in the case. The Kurmis have begun to realize the existence of Chamars.

Data converted in total percentage shown in table exhibit that Bhar respondents (70.71%) are more worried about the dominance of higher castes say Brahmans, Kurmis. Only

21.42% Chamar respondents worry about the dominance of higher castes over them. 5.0% Bhar and 2.85% Chamar respondents do not worry nor do they feel any sort of crisis due to dominance. They refuse to accept higher caste dominance over them.

Table 5.44 (a)

Age (years)	*Yes*	*Class percentage*	*Total percentage*	*No*	*Class percentage*	*Total percentage*	*Total*
15-25	3	75	2.14	1	25	0.71	4
25-35	24	96	17.14	1	4	0.71	25
35-45	45	93.75	32.14	3	6.25	2.14	48
45-55	24	92.30	17.14	2	7.69	1.42	26
55-65	21	84	15	4	16	2.84	25
65-75	10	100.0	7.14	0	0	0	10
75-85	2	100.0	1.42	0	0	0	2
Total	129			11			140

The data placed in table show that 75%, 96%, 93.75%, 92.30%, 84%, 100% and 100% of respondents belonging to age groups 15-25, 25-35, 35-45, 45-55, 55-65, 65-75, and 75-85 respectively feel that higher castes namely Brahmans, Thakurs and Kurmis dominate them. 25%, 4%, 6.25%, 7.69%, 16%, 0% and 0% of respondents belonging to age groups 15-25, 25-35, 35-45, 45-55, 55-65, 65-75 and 75-85 do not feel that higher castes try to dominate or look them down.

The data shown in total percentage indicate that the age group 35-45 is the modal age group of lower caste respondents who have the opinion that higher caste persons look them down or dominate them. 32.14% of respondents belonging to this age group express so. There are two next age groups 25-35 and 45-55 which contain equal number of respondents (17.14% each) who feel that higher castes try to dominate or look down the lower castes say Bhars and Chamars. The age group

75-85 of respondents (1.42%) is least worried about the higher caste dominance in the villages.

Question No. 56

Do the higher caste persons co-operate or go against lower castes ?

Table 5.45

Response	*BH*	*Caste percentage*	*Total percentage*	*CH*	*Class percentage*	*Total percentage*	*Total*
Yes	10	9.43	7.14	0	0	0	10
No	82	77.35	58.57	27	79.41	19.28	109
A	0	0	0	7	17.64	4.28	6
B	0	0	0	1	2.94	0.71	1
C	12	11.32	8.57	0	0	0	12
D	2	1.88	1.42	0	0	0	2
Total	106			34			140

The data shown in table drawn above exhibit that 9.43% of Bhar respondents feel that higher caste persons say Brahmans and Kurmis co-operate them while 77.35% of Bhar respondents feel that the higher castes today go against them. 11.32% of Bhar respondents feel that some members of higher castes cooperate them while some members oppose them. 1.88% of Bhar respondents feel a sense of neutrality on the part of higher castes. They feel that higher caste persons neither cooperate nor go against them. 79.14% of Chamar respondents feel that all the higher castes specially Brahman, Thakur and Kurmi etc. go against them. 17.64% of Chamar respondents opine that higher castes cooperate them due to vested interests and at the moment their interests are fulfilled and needs are satisfied, they go on opposition. 2.94% of Chamar respondents do not need any sort of cooperation from higher castes.

From the data calculated in total percentage, it is obviously understood that a comparatively higher percentage (58.57%) of Bhar respondents in comparison to Chamar respondents (19.28%) realize their opposition by higher castes. However, 7.14% of Bhar respondents also feel a sense of co-operation to them on the part of higher castes. 4.28% of Chamar respondents consider higher caste persons as most cunning in the sense that higher caste persons cooperate lower castes to satisfy their interests and the moment their interests are satisfied they go against them.

Question No. 57

Do the higher caste persons today want to maintain unity and cooperation with lower castes or conflict ?

Table 5.46

Response	*BH*	*Class percentage*	*Total percentage*	*CH*	*Class percentage*	*Total percentage*	*Total*
Yes	10	9.43	7.14	2	5.88	1.42	12
No	82	77.35	58.57	26	76.47	18.57	108
A	0	0	0	6	17.64	4.28	6
C	12	11.32	8.57	0	0	0	12
D	2	1.88	1.42	0	0	0	2
Total	106			34			140

The table shows that 9.43% of Bhar respondents are of the option that higher caste persons want to maintain unity and cooperation with lower castes while 77.35% (a higher percentage) of Bhar respondents feel that higher castes say, Brahmans and Kurmis want to live with conflict. These respondents feel the Brahmans and Kurmis as good conductor of inter-caste tension and conflict. 11.32% of Bhar respondents observe favourable attitude of some of Brahmans and some of Kurmis while at the same time they observe unfavourable attitude of some of Brahmans and some of Kurmis.

Hence, we can formulate a *particular affirmative* proposition that some Brahmans and some Kurmis want to maintain unity and cooperation with lower castes. At the same time, we can formulate a *particular negative* proposition that some Brahmans and some Kurmis do not want to maintain unity and cooperation but rather create conflict-situation with lower castes as expressed by 11.32%. Bhar respondents. 1.88% of Bhar respondents feel neither cooperation nor opposition on the part of higher castes. 5.88% of Chamar respondents observe that the higher castes say Kurmis want to cooperate and maintain unity in the village while 76.47% of Chamar respondents feel that today higher castes do not maintain harmony and unity, rather they intentionally create conflict-situation. 17.64% of Chamar respondents express that in village today the higher castes say Kurmis here cooperate lower castes say Chamars here only because of their vested interests. After the interests being fulfllled they ignore them and behave reversely or negatively.

The data calculated in total percentage reveal that the percentage of Bhar respondents (58.57) who feel that higher castes say Brahman, Thakur and Kurmi create conflict situation with lower castes say Bhars and Chamars, is greater than that of Chamar respondents (67.47%).

Question No. 58

Do the higher caste persons want that the lower castes ought to be given education?

Table 5.47

Response	*BH*	*Class percentage*	*Total percentage*	*CH*	*Class percentage*	*Total percentage*	*Total*
Yes	12	11.32	8.57	3	8.32	2.14	15
No	94	88.67	67.14	31	91.17	22.14	125
Total	106			34			140

The data reveal that 11.32% of Bhar respondeuts feel the liberal attitude of higher castes towards the provision of education to be given to the lower castes, say, Bhar. While a considerably higher number of respondents of the same caste (88.67%) feel that higher castes never think of their education enhancement otherwise who shall work for them. They say that higher castes, say, Brahmans and Kurmis and others, never think of their welfare. They exress, "Brahmans and Kurmis think that if the boys of lower castes get education, who shall, then work for them?" 8.82% of Chamar respondents feel that higher castes favour the educational enhancement of lower caste boys while 91.17% of Chamar respondents do not find the favourable attitude of Brahmans, Thakurs, and Kurmis towards the provision of education to the lower caste boys.

The data converted into total percentage reveal that 8.57% Bhar and 2.14% Chamar respondents observe the favourable attitude of higher castes, viz., Brahmans, Thakurs and Kurmis towards the provision of education to lower castes, viz., Bhars and Chamars while 67.14% Bhar and 22.14% Chamar fail to find such a favourable attitude of higher castes towards lower castes. This is manifest in the village Ashrafpatti (Newada) where some boys of Bhar caste were refused to be admitted in a local Higher Secondary School at Koorki Bazar, Akbarpur (Faizabad) on the special appeal and request of a Brahman teacher of the same school. This Brahman teacher belongs to Panjupur (Newada) village.

The data presented in Table 5.47 (a) show that 25% of respondents belonging to age group 15-25 feel that higher castes favour the provision of education while 75% of respondents of the same age group do not find the favourable attitude of higher castes towards lower castes about the provision of education. 100% of respondents belonging to age group 25-35 feel unfavourable attitude of higher castes. 12.5% of respondents belonging to age group 35-45 feel that higher castes favour the educational enhancement of lower castes while 87.5% of the same age group do not see the favourable attitude of higher ones towards lower ones. 7.69% of respondents of age group 45-55 feel the favourable attitude of higher castes while 92.30% of the same age group do not think so. 24%

Table 5.47 (a)

Age (years)	*Yes*	*Class percentage*	*Total percentage*	*No*	*Class percentage*	*Total perc.n-tage*	*Total*
15-25	1	25	0.71	3	75	2.14	4
25-35	0	0	0	25	100.0	17.85	25
35-45	6	12.5	4.28	42	87.5	30	48
45-55	2	7.69	1.42	24	92.30	17.14	26
55-65	6	24	4.28	19	76	13.57	25
65-75	0	0	0	10	100.0	7.14	10
75-85	0	0	0	2	100.0	1.42	2
Total	15			125			140

respondents of age group 55-65 find the favourable attitude of higher castes while 76% of the same age group hardly find any indication of favourable attitude on the part of higher castes. 100% of respondents belonging to age group 65-75 and the same percentage of respondents belong to 75-85 age group do not find the favourable attitude of higher castes towards lower castes for provision of education. The data indicate that the age groups 25-35, 65-75, and 75-85 are the most hostile age groups as all the members (100%) of each such group observe the unfavourable attitude of higher castes towards the provision to lower ones.

The data converted in total percent, however, give another picture of respondents. Among all age groups, who expressed their negative opinion towards higher castes, the age group 35-45 is most frequented and hence it is a modal hostile age group with a total percent of 30%. Hence, we may pass a concluding remark that among lower caste respondents, the respondents falling in age group 35-45 seem to be most hostile and age group 75-85 a least hostile group.

Question No. 59

Do the higher caste persons give you less wage?

Table 5.48

Response	*BH*	*Class percentage*	*Total percentage*	*CH*	*Class percentage*	*Total percentage*	*Total*
Yes	70	66.03	50	32	94.11	22.85	102
No	35	33.01	25	2	5.88	1.42	37
A	1	0.94	0.71	0	0	0	1
Total	106			34			140

The data presented in table exhibit that 66.03% of Bhars and 94.11% of Chamars feel that they are paid less wage by higher caste land owners. However, only 33.01% of Bhars and 5.88% of Chamars do not feel so. The respondents who do not feel so, may it be because they are busy with their own works and also because they get what they demand. 0.94% of Bhar respondent expresses that he shall not like to go to higher castes to work. The total percentage of Bhar respondents (50%) is higher than that of Chamar respondents (22.85%) while affirming the question. Similarly, the total percentage of Bhar respondents (25%) is again greater than that of Chamar respondents (1.42%) while negating the question. Since the majority of Bhar and Chamar respondents realize the tendency of higher castes who pay less wage, we assume that higher castes exploit the lower castes which may lead to caste-conflict between higher and lower. (Table 5.49)

The table shows that 40.56% of Bhar and 88.23% of Chamar respondents feel that Brahmans and Kurmis have illegally ploughed Chak-road and have unauthorisedly captured the lands like 'Usar', 'Banjar', and habilitable lands of Bhars and Chamars. 59.43% of Bhar and 11.76% of Chamar respondents, however, do not observe such mis-acts of Brahmans and Kurmis.

Question No. 60

Is it true that higher caste persons are taking the benefit of lands of lower castes ?

Table 5.49

Response	*BH*	*Class percent-age*	*Total percent-age*	*CH*	*Class percent-age*	*Total percent-age*	*Total*
Yes	43	40.56	30.71	30	88.23	21.42	73
No	63	59.43	45	4	11.76	2.85	67
Total	106			34			140

The total percentage of Bhars (30.7%) who find that higher castes are taking the benefit of lands of lower castes is greater than that of Chamar respondents (21.42%). 45% (total percentage) of Bhars and 2.85% (total percentage) of Chamar respondents do not find such a case in the village.

A comparison of class percentage of respondents shows that only 40.56% of Bhar respondents in comparison to 88.23% of Chamar respondents observe the lands being illegally captured by higher castes. Therefore, Chamar respondents are more aggrieved of higher castes.

Question No. 61

Opinion of respondents about the assaults of lower castes by higher castes.

Table 5.50

Response	*BH*	*Class percent-age*	*Total percent-age*	*CH*	*Class percent-age*	*Total percent-age*	*Total*
Yes	9	8.49	6.42	0	0	0	9
No	97	91.50	69.28	34	100.0	24.28	131
Total	106			34			140

The table shows that only 8.49% of Bhar respondents express that the lower castes should be assaulted by higher castes such as beating or abusing them only if they commit mistakes otherwise not. 91.50% of respondents drawn from the same caste consider it improper to abuse or beat the lower castes on part of higher castes. 100% of Chamar respondents also condemn the mal-acts, like beating or abusing, by higher castes to lower castes. Both Bhar and Chamar respondents in greatest magnitude consider the assaults as inhuman, filthy, improper, and illegal. They never think that higher castes should assault lower castes. Here, it may be concluded that lower castes today have lost the capacity and courage to tolerate the mischievous acts of higher castes. In case it happens so, they will be more hostile towards higher castes.

Question No. 62

Is it true or false that the higher castes take the benefit from lower castes through trickery ?

Table 5.51

Response	*BH*	*Class percentage*	*Total percentage*	*CH*	*Class percentage*	*Total percentage*	*Total*
Yes	73	68.86	52.14	32	94.11	22.85	105
No	33	31.13	23.57	2	5.88	1.42	35
Total	106			34			140

The data show that 68.86% of Bhar and 94.11% of Chamar respondents opine that higher castes, say, Brahmans and Kurmis are tricksters and they always try their best to take the benefit on the cost of lower castes viz., Bhars and Chamars. The Bhar respondents of Rabipur Bahauddinpur village express that the Brahmans of this village take money from them pretending to provide them agricultural land (money on 'Rehan') but later on, they prohibit them to go in field (Khet men pair mat rakkho). 31.13% of Bhar and 5.88% of Chamar respondents reveal that Brahmans and Kurmis always seek Bhars and Chamars to take benefit from them through trickery but they fail to do so and get nothing as the Bhars and Chamars have come to know the tricks of Brahmans and Kurmis and therefore, they are aware of them.

The total percentage of Bhars and Chamars who answer in affirmative show that 52.14% and 22.85% respectively while those who answer negatively show that 23.57% and 1.42% respectively [Table 5.51 (a)].

Table 5.51 (a)

Age (years)	*Yes*	*Class percent-age*	*Total percent-age*	*No*	*Class percent-age*	*Total percent-age*	*Total*
15-25	2	50	1.42	2	50	1.42	4
25-35	22	88	15.71	3	12	2.14	25
35-45	36	75	25.71	12	25	8.57	48
45-55	19	73.07	13.57	7	26.92	5	26
55-65	15	60	10.71	10	40	7.14	25
65-75	9	90	6.42	1	10	0.71	10
75-85	2	100.0	1.42	0	0	0	2
Total	105			35			140

The table shows that the respondents lying in age group 15-25 bifurcate in two sub-groups of equal size (50% in each sub-group). One sub-group feels that higher castes take the benefits from lower castes through trickery while other sub-group refutes this fact. 88% of respondents lying in age group 25-35, 75% lying in age group 35-45, 73.07% lying in age group 45-55, 60% lying in age 55-65, 90% lying in age group 65-75 and 100% lying in age group 75-85 confirm the hypothesis that higher caste persons (say, Brahmans and Kurmis) take the benefits from lower castes (say, Bhar and Chamar) through trickery. While 12%, 25%, 26.92%, 40%, 10% and 0% of respondents lying in age groups 25-35, 35-45, 45-55, 55-65, 65-75 and 75-85 respectively refute the hypothesis. It is from the table, therefore, clear that majority of the respondents answering in affirmative approve the hypothesis. However, the age group 35-45 being highly frequented is modal age group of lower castes with a class percentage of 75% and total percentage of 25.71% who feel that higher castes are tricksters and they try to cheat the lower castes and enjoy.

Table 5.51 (b)

Education	*Yes*	*Class percentage*	*Total percentage*	*No*	*Class percentage*	*Total percentage*	*Total*
Illiterates	75	75.75	53.57	24	24.24	17.14	99
Nominally educated	30	75	21.42	10	25	7.14	40
Highly educated	0	0	0	1	100.0	0.71	1
Total	105			35			140

The data shown in table exhibit that 75.75% illiterate respondents observe that higher castes take the benefit from lower castes. 24.24% of illiterate respondents do not think so. 75% nominally educated respondents think so. Zero percent of highly educated respondents think so while 100% of highly educated respondents observe that higher castes fail to do so. The table also shows that in comparison to nominally educated respondents, illiterate respondents have more negative opinion towards higher castes and consider them as trickster. The total percentage of illiterate respondents (53.57%) as compared to that of nominally educated respondents (21.42%) also indicates the same result. Hence, illiterate respondents are more hostile and have more negative attitude towards higher castes.

Table 5.51 (c) at a glance reveals the fact that 75.82% of respondents belonging to nuclear family express that the higher caste persons, say, Brahman, Kayastha, Kurmi, etc., take the benefits from them through trickery. 24.17% of respondents belonging to same family type do not feel so. 73.46% of lower caste respondents belonging to joint family express that

Table 5.51 (c)

Family Type	*Yes*	*Class percentage*	*Total percentage*	*No*	*Class percentage*	*Total percentage*	*Total*
Nuclear	69	75.82	49.28	22	24.17	15.71	91
Joint	36	73.46	25.71	13	26.53	9.28	49
Total	105			35			140

the h'gher caste persons take benefit from them through trickery. However, 26.53% of respondents living in joint family do not think so.

The total percentage of above data indicate that a largest percentage of respondents living in nuclear family feel that higher caste persons take the benefits from lower caste persons. Th's negative attitude and observation of lower caste respondents is positively correlated with tension and/or conflict between higher and lower castes (Table 5.52).

Question No. 63

Do higher castes commit injustice with lower castes ?

Table 5.52

Response	*BH*	*Class percentage*	*Total percentage*	*CH*	*Class percentage*	*Total percentage*	*Total*
Yes	62	58.49	44.28	32	94.11	22.85	94
No	44	41.50	21.42	2	5.88	1.42	46
Total	106			34			140

The data show that 58.49% of Bhar and 94.11% of Chamar respondents observe that Brahmans and Kurmis because of casteism disfavour Bhars and Chamar and they commit injustice with them. 41.50% of Bhar respondents and 5.88% of Chamar respondents, however, do not observe such step on the part of higher castes.

The Bhar respondents of Rabipur Bahauddinpur village who answer in negative opine that Brahmans and Kurmis of the village fail to commit injustice with them because of the organization of Bhar caste (Hamare Sangathan Ke Aage Unhen Neecha Dikhana Parata Hai). The total percentages of Bhar and Chamar respondents who answer in affirmative are 44.28% and 22.85% respectively. And that who answer in negative are 31.42% and 1.42% for Bhars and Chamars respectively.

Table 5.52 (a)

Age (years)	*Yes*	*Class percent-age*	*Total percent-age*	*No*	*Class percent-age*	*Total percent-age*	*Total*
15-25	2	50	1.42	2	50	1.42	4
25-35	32	88	15.71	3	12	2.14	25
35-45	30	62.5	21.42	18	37.5	12.85	48
45-55	11	42.30	7.85	15	57.69	10.71	26
55-65	19	76	13.57	6	24	4.28	25
65-75	8	80	5.71	2	20	1.42	10
75-85	2	100.0	1.42	0	0	0	2
Total	94			46			140

The table shows that in comparison to all other age groups, the age group 75-85 has maximum class percentage (100%). Next are 25-35, 65-75 and 55-65 age groups with 88%, 80% and 76% respectively who approve the hypothesis that higher castes commit injustice with lower castes. In spite of the above facts the age group 35-45 because of having maximum number of respondents is most frequented and hence is a modal age group with class percentage of 62.5% who approve the statement that higher castes commit injustice with lower castes. In comparison to other age groups, 35-45 age group has maximum total percentage of 21.42%. At this point, we may, therefore, conclude that the lower caste respondents of age group 35-45 have more negative attitude towards higher castes.

Question No. 64

Is it true that some persons take the benefit of ignorance of lower castes ?

Table 5.53

Response	*BH*	*Class percentage*	*Total percentage*	*CH*	*Class percentage*	*Total percentage*	*Total*
Yes	72	67.92	51.42	30	88.23	21.42	102
No	34	32.07	24.28	4	11.76	2.85	38
Total	106			34			140

The data shown in table exhibit that 67.92% of Bhar respondents observe that Brahmans, Kurmis and Kayasthas ignore them from government facilities say financial supports through Block. These respondents feel that the higher castes considar them fool and take hard work and in lieu thereof they pay less amount. The higher castes do not loose the opportunity if they get or if it is within their power. They try their best to enjoy all the facilities they can. 88.23% of Chamar respondents belonging to Hazipur Marui village observe that Brahmans, Thakurs and Kurmis of the village as well as of locality pay them less amount of wage. These higher castes enjoy half of the amount obtained through 'Antyodaya' scheme and pay only half to the Chamars of the village. Because of being in power, the higher caste persons always try to put Chamars in dark. Also, to achieve power, they put them in dark (Satta Men Bane Rahne Ke Prayojana Se Ye Hame Andhere Men Dalane Ka Prayash Karate Hain).

The total percentage of Bhar respondents (51.42%) who answer in affirmative and confirm the hypothesis, is greater than the total percentage of Chamar respondents (21.42%). Similarly the total percentage of Bhar respondents (24.28%), who refute the hypothesis is also greater than the total percentage of Chamar respondents (2.85%).

However the respondents who answer in negative are of the opinion that the higher castes try to take the benefit of ignorance of lower castes but they fail to do so. Hence, on the grounds of benefits of ignorance, the lower caste respondents have negative attitude towards higher castes which is positively correlated with inter-caste tension between higher and lower castes.

Question No. 65

May the lower castes take revenge from higher castes if they get chance ?

Table 5.54

Response	*BH*	*Class percent-age*	*Total percent-age*	*CH*	*Class percent-age*	*Total percent-age*	*Total*
Yes	78	73.58	55.71	33	97.05	23.57	111
No	24	22.64	17.14	1	2.94	0.71	25
A	3	2.83	2.14	0	0	0	3
B	1	0.94	0.71	0	0	0	1
Total	106			34			140

The table shows that 73.58% of Bhar respondents are of the opinion that they may take revenge from higher castes if they get chance. However, 22.64% of respondents of the same caste do not think so. 2.83% of the respondents are of the opinion that they believe in peace and satisfaction. But if the opposite castes press them, they shall automatically be bound to come on front. 0.94% of respondent of the same caste also opines that he does not think of revenge (Ham Badala Lene Kee Bhavana Nahin Rakhate hain). Being bound he can take revenge from higher castes. 97.05% of Chamar respondents agree to take revenge while a considerably smallest percentage (2.94%) of the respondents of same caste disagree to take revenge. The respondents of Rabipur Bahauddinpur village who do not believe in revenge say that he who stops his step immediately after demoralizing the enemy is the man in real sense. (Mard Vah hai Jo Dushman Ke Kayal Hone Par Apana Kadam Vahin Rok De). The Bhar respondents of Panjupur (Newada) and Ashrafpatti (Newada) say that they are small men, how can they take revenge from higher castes ?

Question No. 66

Do the higher caste persons take the unauthorized benefit of their superiority from lower castes ?

Table 5.55

Response	*BH*	*Class percent-age*	*Total percent-age*	*CH*	*Class percent-age*	*Total percent-age*	*Total*
Yes	52	49.05	37.14	29	28.29	20.71	81
No	54	50.94	38.57	5	14.70	3.57	59
Total	106			34			140

The data shown in table drawn above indicate that 49.05% of Bhar and 28.29% of Chamar respondents feel that Brahmans and Kurmis take the unauthorized and illegal benefit of their superiority from them. They express that Brahmans and Kurmis take hard work and in lieu thereof they provide a very little amount of wage to them. They have ploughed Chak-road illegally. They have pressed Assistant Chakbandi Officer to throw the lands of lower castes distant and provide them waste lands viz., 'Usar', and 'Banjar'. They try to beat or abuse not only them but to the guests of lower castes also. They try to capture lands of lower castes illegally and harm the crops on demand of higher and proper wage in such a period of crisis.

From Table 5.55 (a) it is obvious that the age group 35-45 is made having maximum number of respondents who are divided in two camps on the basis of difference of opinion. One group of respondents (52.08%) express that higher caste

Table 5.55 (a)

Age (years)	*Yes*	*Class percent-age*	*Total percent-age*	*No*	*Class percent-age*	*Total percent-age*	*Total*
15-25	2	50	1.42	2	50	1.42	4
25-35	21	84	15	4	16	2.84	25
35-45	25	52.08	17.85	23	47.91	16.42	48
45-55	15	57.69	10.71	11	42.30	7.85	26
55-65	12	48	8.57	13	52	9.28	25
65-75	5	50	3.57	5	50	3.57	10
75-85	1	50	0.71	1	50	0.71	2
Total	81			59			140

persons take the benefit of their superiority while other group (47.91%) refutes this fact. However, since the percentage of accepters is greater than refuters, we conclude that majority of respondents belonging to age group 35-45 have negative attitude towards the higher castes as the latter impose their superiority upon former. Also they abuse and threat the lower castes. They try to take debts in the name of lower caste persons. They want to take more work without wage by threatening them. They hate lower castes on the basis of caste feelings. 50.94% of Bhar and 14.70% of Chamar respondents do not, however, feel such activities on the part of higher castes.

The total percentage of Bhar respondents (37.14%) who feel that higher caste persons, say, Brahmans and Kurmis take the unauthorized benefit of their superiority from lower castes, is greater than the total percentage of Chamar respondents (20.71%) which indicate that Bhars in comparison to Chamars are more aggrieved of higher castes. 38.57% of Bhar and 3.57% of Chamar respondents, however, do not feel so. [Table 5.55 (b)].

The data shown in table highlight the facts that 59.59% of illterats respondents observe that higher caste persons viz.,

Table 5.55 (b)

Education	*Yes*	*Class percentage*	*Total percentage*	*No*	*Class percentage*	*Total percentage*	*Total*
Illiterates	59	59.59	42.14	40	40.40	28.57	99
Nominally Educated	22	55	15.71	18	45	12.85	40
Highly Educated	0	0	0	1	100.0	0.71	1
Total	81			59			140

Brahmans and Kurmis take the benefits of their superiority from lower castes. 40.40% of respondents belonging to same educational class category do not observe so. 55% of nominally educated respondents also feel that higher caste persons because of their superiority achieve so many facilities and benefits while 45% of respondents belonging to the same category and 100% of respondents belonging to highly educated class category do not feel so. From analysis of data, it appears that illiterate respondents here are more hostile towards higher castes. Nominally educated respondents are less hostile and highly educated respondents are most liberal towards higher castes. The total percentage of respondents of different category also confirm the hypothesis that illiterate respondents (42.14%) as compared to nominally educated (15.71%) and highly educated (0.0%) respondents have more negative opinion towards higher castes. Hence the conflict in villages today is more observable between illiterate lower castes and higher castes than between other educational categories of lower castes and higher castes. Here, we may, therefore, pass a concluding remark that higher the education, more shall be the chances of warmth relation between higher and lower castes and lesser the education more the chances of conflict between higher and lower castes.

The data shown in Table 5.55 (c) exhibit that 59.34% and 55.10% of respondents living in nuclear and joint families respectively feel that higher caste persons take the unautho-

Table 5.55 (c)

Family Types	*Yes*	*Class percent-age*	*Total percent-age*	*No*	*Class percent-age*	*Total percent-age*	*Total*
Nuclear	54	59.34	38.57	37	40.65	26.42	91
Joint	27	55.10	19.28	22	44.89	15.71	49
Total	81			59			140

rized benefit of their superiority from low caste persons. However, 40.65% and 44.89% of respondents belonging to nuclear and joint families respectively do not observe so.

The total percentage of above data indicate that in comparison to respondents belonging to joint family (19.28%), the respondents belonging to nuclear family (38.57%) have more negative attitude towards higher caste persons. Hence we may pass a concluding remark that the majority of lower caste persons (say, Bhar and Chamar) belonging to nuclear family carry on a greater proportion of momentum of tension and give rise to inter-caste tension and conflict between higher and lower castes.

Conclusion

On the basis of findings of Tables 55, 55 (a), 55 (b) and 55 (c), we may conclude that illiterate lower caste respondents belonging to age group 35-45 and living in nuclear family have more negative attitude towards higher castes and they are directly responsible for inter-caste tension in village today.

Question No. 67

Is it true that lower caste persons shall not get sufficient grain even after doing hard work?

Researcher taking an interview with a Bhar respondent of village Rabipur Bahauddinpur.

Table 5.56

Response	*BH*	*Class percentage*	*Total percentage*	*CH*	*Class percentage*	*Total percentage*	*Total*
Yes	0	0	0	14	41.17	10	14
No	106	100.0	75.71	20	58.82	14.28	126
Total	106			34			140

The table shows that 100% of Bhar respondents disagree with such a view that thy shall not get sufficient grain to eat even after a hard work. Our Bhar respondents are not pessimist nor do they depend upon fate. They believe in work and they express that they shall surely get sufficient grain to eat by the way of hard work. They feel that the taste of hard work is sweet. The hard work shall surely provide them sufficient to eat. 41.17% of Chamar respondents, on the other side, opine that the higher caste persons even after taking hard work do not pay proper wage and therefore the question of getting sufficient grain to eat does tot arise. However, 58.82%

of Chamar respondents believe in hard work and say that they shall surely enjoy the life by the way of doing hard work.

The total percentage of Bhar respondents who approve the hypothesis that it is true that lower caste persons shall not get sufficient grain to eat even after doing hard work, is zero while that of Chamar respondents is 10%. The total percentage of Bhar respondents who refute the hypothesis is 75.71% and that of Chamar respondents is 14.28%. The data also show that the Bhar respondents are more optimist than Chamar respondents.

Question No. 68

Do the higher caste persons want that lower caste persons should get enough grain to eat and enjoy a happy life or not?

Table 5.57

Response	*BH*	*Class percent-age*	*Total percent-age*	*CH*	*Class percent-age*	*Total percent-age*	*Total*
Yes	3	2.83	2.14	2	5.88	1.42	5
No	103	97.16	73.57	32	94.11	22.85	135
Total	106			34			140

From the data given in above table, it is clear that 2.83% of Bhar respondents express their opinon that higher caste persons want them to enjoy a happy life while 97.16% of Bhar respondents feel that higher caste persons never want their welfare. For example, when faction formed in the village Rabipur Bahauddinpur, the Brahmans and Kurmis of the village refused Bhars to give water for crop-irrigation. It indicates that higher caste persons never want the welfare of lower castes. 5.88% of Chamar respondents feel that higher caste persons want them to lead a happy life while 94.11% of respondents of the same caste have negative opinion towards higher castes.

In the light of above data, it is found that the majority of respondents belonging to Bhar and Chamar castes has negative opinion towards higher castes and hence there is inter-caste tension between higher and lower castes today.

The total percentage of Bhar respondents who have positive opinion towards higher castes is 2.14% and that of Chamar is 1.42%. On the other hand, the total percentage of Bhar respondents who have negative opinion towards higher castes is 73.57% and that of Chamar is 22.85% The total percentage of Bhar respondents, who have negative opinion towards higher castes, being more than three times greater than that of Chamar respondents indicates that Bhars are more hostile than Chamars towards higher castes.

Table 5.57 (a)

Age (years)	*Yes*	*Class percent-age*	*Total percent-age*	*No*	*Class percent-age*	*Total percent-age*	*Total*
15-25	1	25	0.71	3	75	2.14	4
25-35	0	0	0	25	100.0	17.85	25
35-45	2	4.16	1.42	46	95.83	32.85	48
45-55	0	0	0	26	100.0	18.57	26
55-65	1	4	0.71	24	96	17.14	25
65-75	1	10	0.71	9	90	6.42	10
75-85	0	0	0	2	100.0	1.42	2
Total	5			135			140

The table shows that maximum number of respondents (95.83%), who feel that higher caste persons do not want the welfare of lower castes, fall in age group 35-45. The total percentage of these respondents is 32.85% being greatest of all. Hence age group 35-45 is the modal hostile group whose members carry much of conflict momentum with them and are predicted to be most hostile in future towards higher cates. They are creator of conflict situation and cleavage.

On the group level, the age groups 25-35, 45-55 and 75-85 are although, more hostile than other age groups as each of them shows a class percentage of 100 and has a negative opinion towards higher castes, but because of being less in number in whole universe under study, has less total percent and therefore, these groups lag behind in whole universe in comparison to age group 35-45 which has the greatest total percent. Hence, it is proved that 35-45 age group is most hostile modal age group and whose members contain more momentum of conflict which is positively correlated with the tension and/or conflict between higher and lower castes, (Table 5.58)

Question No. 69

Do your castemen obey higher castes due to fear or because they think that the order of higher castes is right and proper?

Table 5.58

Response	*BH*	*Class percent-age*	*Total percent-age*	*CH*	*Class percent-age*	*Total percent-age*	*Total*
A	23	21.69	16.42	0	0	0	23
B	13	12.26	9.28	5	14.70	3.57	18
C	5	4.71	3.57	0	0	0	5
D	5	4.71	3.57	1	2.94	0.71	6
E	4	3.77	2.85	0	0	0	4
F	3	2.83	2.14	28	82.35	20	31
G	1	0.94	0.71	0	0	0	1
H	1	0.94	0.71	0	0	0	1
No	51	48.11	36.42	0	0	0	51
Total	106			34			140

The data shown in table throw light on the facts that 21.69% of Bhar respondents obey higher castes due to morality and behaviour and also due to the sentiments of brotherly relation. 12.26% of respondents follow and obey the true orders and true things of higher castes. 4.71% of respondents obey only those men of higher castes who are of strong moral character. The same percentage of respondents (4.71%) obey them considering their order as right and proper. 3.77% obey them due to their superiority. 2.83% obey them due to fear. 0.94% believes in 'tit for tat'. 0.9% behave on the indication of his castemen. However, 48.11% of Bhar respondents disobey higher caste persons.

The accounts of data on Chamar respondents are given here. 14.70% of Chamer respondents obey higher caste persons on genuine grounds. 2.94% obey them considering their order as right and proper. 82.35% obey them due to their fear. The remarkable point lies here in the fact that there is not a single case of Chamar who has a clear-cut opinion of disobedience. In one way or other, mostly they seem to obey their superior castes in the village. However, approximately half of the Bhar respondents (48.11%) clearly refuse to obey the law and order of their superior castes, say Brahmans, Kurmis and Kayasthas.

Out of Bhar respondents who obey higher castes, maximum class percentage (21.69) is of those respondents who obey due to behaviour and sentimental association of brotherly relation. On the other hand, majority of Chamar respondents (82.35% obey the superior castes due to fear. From this, it is derived that the amount of fear from higher castes is more in Chamar caste than that in Bhar caste. However, the Chamar caste is slightly more bold (14.70%) than Bhar caste (12.26%) as they obey only true order of higher ones.

Data in total percentage give us a slightly different picture of the responses. Being all the generalization static, we find but one new and different statement that in universe as a whole, the total percentage of Bhar respondents (9.28%) who obey only true and genuine order of superior castes is greater than that of Chamar respondents (3.57%). By this, we revise our statement that on the universe level, the Bhars are slightly more bold than the Chamars. (Table 5.59).

Question No. 70

Do lower castes not sit on cot in presence of higher castes because of their fear or because of their superiority?

Table 5.59

Response	*BH*	*Class percent-age*	*Total percent-age*	*CH*	*Class percent-age*	*Total percent-age*	*Total*
A	8	7.54	5.71	0	0	0	8
C	4	3.77	2.85	0	0	0	4
E	6	5.66	4.28	0	0	0	6
F	0	0	0	27	79.41	19.28	27
G	3	2.83	2.14	0	0	0	3
I	85	80.18	60.71	7	20.58	5	92
Total	106			34			140

The data presented in table highlight that 7.54% of Bhar respondents do not sit on cot in presence of Brahmans and Kurmis due to individual behaviour and brotherhood. 3.77% of Bhar respondents welcome and respect those higher caste persons who bear precise manner and excellent moral character. 5.66% of Bhar respondents consider higher castes as superior. 2.83%, however, behave according to the principle of 'Tit for Tat'. 80.18% of Bhar respondents do not get down from cot when a higher caste person comes or remains there. They say that the old custom of getting down from cot or not to sit on cot in presence of higher caste persons has today gone to extinction. Though, older generation of lower castes continue and practice the old custom of cot while younger generation does not practice it.

A considerably higher percentage of Chamar respondents (79.41%) respect the higher caste and leave the cot due to fear while 20.58% of same caste respondents maintain the social relationship of equality with Kurmi caste in village and sit on cot even in their presence.

The data indicate that the majority of Chamar respondents is feeling a sense of fear from the side of Kurmis while Bhar respondents are quite fearless (zero percent) from the side of Brahmans and Kurmis. This is because of more population and more unity within the Bhar caste community. The Bhar respondents (2.83) enjoy the principle of 'Tit-for-Tat' while Chamar respondents indicate zero percent on this point.

Conclusion

In the light of above data, we may pass a concluding remark that the sense of superiority of and fear from higher caste is loosing its significance in village today and the rural lower caste persons have begun to march from older custom of leaving the cot in presence of higher caste persons to modern custom of social equality. This is an indication of social change in rural lower caste population which is threatening the prestige of higher caste persons. The way to snatch the prestige of higher castes has really created a nuisance, cleavage and conflict between higher and lower castes.

Question No. 71

If you are not afraid of higher castes then why ?

Table 5.60

Response	*BH*	*Class percentage*	*Total percentage*	*CH*	*Class percentage*	*Total percentage*	*Total*
A	6	5.66	4.28	6	17.64	4.28	12
B	2	1.88	1.42	0	0	0	2
C	1	0.94	0.71	25	73.52	17.85	26
D	57	53.77	40.71	0	0	0	57
E	0	0	0	1	2.94	0.71	1
G	40	37.73	28.57	0	0	0	40
NR	0	0	0	2	5.88	1.42	2

The data shown in table indicate that 5.66% of Bhar respondents feel that they have got a strong unity in and strong organization of own caste, therefore, they do not fear from higher castes, say Brahmans, Kurmis and Kayasthas. 1.88% feel that human behaviour is observable with respect to time and space. The former changes with a change in latter. 0.94% feels that he fears from those who bear excellent moral character. 53.77% enjoy economic independence. They earn and eat. They do not run into debts of Brahmans, Kurmis and Kayasthas and therefore, they enjoy a free, frank and fearless style of life. 37.73% feel fearless on the ground of their economic independence and success in village election.

The account of data on Chamar respondents is also presented here. 17.64% of Chamar respondents enjoy a fearless life due to their caste unity and solidarity. However, a considerably higher percentage of Chamar respondents feel fear from those of higher castes who bear excellent character. 2.94% think that life is a battle. Therefore, they have lost the sense of fear.

Question No. 72

Do you understand yourself protected from higher castes ?

Table 5.61

Response	*BH*	*Class percent-age*	*Total percent-age*	*CH*	*Class percent-age*	*Total percent-age*	*Total*
Yes	54	50.94	38.57	8	23.52	5.71	62
No	52	49.05	37.14	26	76.47	18.57	78
Total	106			34			140

The data shown in above table exhibit that 50.94% of Bhar respondents feel that they have got their caste organization and have more numerical strength in village, therefore higher caste persons belonging to Brahman and Kurmi caste shall not harm them while 49.05% of Bhar respondents feel themselves unsecured and unprotected from the sides of higher castes. These respondents are of the opinion that there is no guarantee of good behaviour of higher castes. Higher castes being trickster may harm and attack over them at any time. 23.52% of Chamar respondents feel themselves safe and secured from the side of higher castes specially from the side of Kurmi caste while 76.47% of respondents belonging to Chamar caste opine that they are insecured and unsafe from the side of higher castes (Kurmi—say). The total percentage of respondents are like this. 38.57% of Bhar and 5.71% of Chamar respondents feel safe and secured while 37.14% of Bhar and 18.57% of Chamar respondents feel themselves insecured and that they can be attacked by higher castes or put into crisis by them at any time and at any space. In the light of above data it is concluded that in comparison to Chamar respondents, Bhar respondents are acutely closed to uncertainty and contingency and they feel of more oppression on part of external force caused by higher caste persons.

Reasons of Inter-Caste Tension and Conflict

A. Behaviour of higher castes towards lower castes:

1. Imposition of superiority by Brahmans and Kurmis upon Bhars and Chamars.
2. Use of abusive languages, beating, assaulting the ladies of lower caste (Bhar) when their cattles go in the harvest of higher castes.
3. To prohibit Bhars not to cut grass in Brahman's field.
4. To compel Bhars and Chamars to do more work.
5. To order Bhars to do a series of works.
6. To threat the esteem and prestige of Bhars and Chamars and their guests.
7. To be jealous of fashionable dress of lower caste youths.
8. To expect of lower castes to get down from cot and not to sit on cot in their presence.
9. Unnecessary dominance.

10. To pass remarks and comments upon those lower caste persons who try to attend the public meetings of a leader.
11. To pay less than minimum wage.
12. To organize (Brahmans and Kurmis of Hazipur Marui village) against Bhars when a Kurmi candidate got defeated and a Bhar candidate got won as village president.
13. To discooperate Bhars at all stages.
14. To take the benefits of ignorance of Bhars and Chamars. That is, to digest nearly half of the amount financed for poor castes under 'Antyodaya' scheme.
15. To capture lands illegally. To plough the 'Banjar', 'Usar' and Chak-roads unauthorizedly. To capture the land of 'Gram-Samaj' by Kurmis of Hazipur Marui.
16. To disallow the lower castes not to pass through their fields. This was observed in village Rabipur Bahauddinpur by Kurmi and in village Panjupur (Newada) by Brahmans.

B. Behaviour of lower castes towards higher castes:

1. To ignore the higher castes.
2. To threat the prestige of higher castes.
3. To work less and demand higher wage.
4. To discooperate the Brahmans and Kurmis and refuse not to work in their agricultural fields.
5. To disobey them.
6. To show to emerge as a dominant caste (Bhar) and to gain political power as is obvious in village Rabipur Bahauddinpur.
7. To organize to fight against Brahmans and Kurmis as is visible in almost all the villages. Bhars of Ashrafpatti (Newada) with the co-operation of Bhars of Panjupur (Newada) met conflicting situation and beat a Brahman who expired after a

little duration. The Bhars of Rabipur Bahauddinpur also used abusive language to a Brahman on the matter of a dog-bite. The Chamars of Hazipur Marui lodged a writ against Kurmi and were declared successful by lower court, Faizabad, U.P.

8. Bhars and Chamars in their villages are showing a state of fearlessness from Brahmans and Kurmis.
9. They maintain their caste solidarity and think it as the strongest alternative to survive and fight against opponent higher castes.
10. They have become out of higher caste's control.
11. Favourable provision of legal security has made the lower caste persons (Chamar) to enjoy a free, frank and fearless life which is endangering the prestigious position of higher castes in village today.
12. They have started sitting on cot even in the presence of higher castes. They respect only those who are men of high moral character.
13. They shirk and work wilfully and avoid the order of higher castes.
14. They have got their own caste-leaders and do not want the interference of higher castes in their matters.
15. They do not have high perception about higher castes.
16. They think that higher caste persons do not wish them best. The Bhars of Ashrafpatti (Newada) are much dissatified by the behaviour of Brahmans of Panjupur (Newada) when they came to know that a High School teacher of Panjupur (Newada) belonging to Brahman caste appealed and approached the Principal of the local school not to write the name of a Bhar boy.
17. Lower caste persons (Bhars) intentionally show social, cultural, economic and political activities

parallel to Brahmans with a view to dominate. This picture is clear in Ashrafpatti (Newada).

18. The younger generation of both Bhar and Chamar castes claim to be of similar rank and social status and even they try to reduce the status of higher castes.

6

Conclusion

Modern social world is charactarized by conflict. Conflict prevails in almost all sectors of human life. It starts from birth and ends in death. Truly, Vivekanands has spoken of life as a struggle. In his own words, Life is struggle, let me die fighting. In multi India, different social grousps are struggling with each other. The processes of social differentiation and social stratification have disturbed the whole human world. Scarcity of social values have led the social beings to enter the competitive market. Every individual of the society desires to share these values. In sharing of these scarce social values, the individuals compete with each other. In competition, if they find their failure, they adopt the other strategy. The strategy applied often gives rise to conflict. This phenomenon is observed at group level also. The different social groups want to share these values. The looser group often meets conflict-situation against gainer-group. Even, during the process of gain of the values, the different groups may meet conflict-situation.

The present study has been an humble attempt at understanding the pattern of conflict prevailing between different castes. How was this phenomenon as sociologically problematic was due to the fact that the forward-backward conflict in Akbarpur was generally heard from the mouihs of all the men of the locality. Not only this, but it was popular at State of Uttar Pradesh level even. Therefore, we thought it to deal with and hence, proposed to understand from sociological point of view. This Doctoral Dissertation is an outcome of the present study based on field data on rural people. The other rationale of selection of this problem lies in the fact that very least studies have been conducted in this area of research.

In all, four villages have been purposively selected as the intensity of conflict in these villages is observed acute. These are: (i) Panjupur (Newada), Ashraf Patti (Newada), Rabipur Bahauddinpur and Hazipur Marui. These all lie within the circumference of Akbarpur block. The different caste groups in these villages are in conflict situation. For instance, there is conflict between Brahman of Panjupur (Newada) and Bhar of Ashrafpatti (Newada). This is characterized as inter-village forward-backward caste conflict. There is also conflict in village Rabipur Bahauddinpur mainly between two castes i.e., Kurmi and Bhar, while a third but higher caste (Brahman) is also involved, and the caste conflict ultimately takes the form of factionalism. This conflict may chiefly be characterized as intra-village intra-backward conflict. Furthermore, there is conflict between Kurmi and Chamar in the village Hazipur Marui, and hence, it is intra-village backward-scheduled caste conflict. These three models were taken into account to analyse them sociologically. The respondents were selected through the application of Census method and in this way, all the respondents were the male househeads of these castes. In all, 200 respondents were interviewed with the help of an interview schedule containing 34 questions in common and 18 questions for comparatively higher and 20 for low castes separately. Besides these, the three other techniques are also used for the collection of data which are observation, group interview and case study. Group interview technique is one kind of interview technique. This technique, as we feel, is most useful for quicker response in shorter period. The data collected mainly with the help of interview schedule were tabulated and numerous of tables were formed. In this thesis, the tables for those responses have been generally not drawn in which all the respondents have given their perfect agreement. However, the tables showing varying responses have been shown frequently. The use of simple calculation of percentage is frequently visible in the thesis.

The nature of conflict characterizing the different castes in our villages has grown out of life style woven around the scarce social values like power, prestige, influence and resources. The Brahmans and Kurmis have exercised their influence in a great magnitude over Bhars and Chamars, because the land has been the main source of Brahmans and Kurmis to gain wealth and political power. The higher position of Brahmans and Kurmis in the villages has also found support in old values of traditional Indian caste system which confers to some castes inherent superiority over other castes.

The inter-caste relationship which exists in our villages is due to the facts that different castes threat the prestige of others. This threat is practiced enormously by higher castes over lower castes due to their inherent superiority since tradition. In response to this threat, the lower castes have also begun to threat the prestige of higher ones, as is evident in all the villages under study.

The desire of sharing and enjoying political power in independent rural India by different castes is an emerging trend in human behaviour. This is most obviously visible in Rabipur Bahauddinpur and Harzipur Marui villages. Before independence, there was no provision and hard-fast rule for the maintenance of socio-political equality. The powers were in the hands of land owing higher castes. Independent India Government has adopted different Constitutional measures to remove social discriminations and bring out equality. Furthermore, the fundamental rights of all human-beings are reserved in every sphere of social life. In this social condition, specially lower castes (backwards and scheduled castes) have started entering the competitive market. Snatching of polititical power by lower castes and schduled castes from the hands of pre-dominant power group has opened a new arena of conflict between power-seekers and power-enjoyers as is evident in these villages.

The payment of very low wages to the Bhar agricultural workers by land owing Brahman caste and order them continuously to do a series of works; and in case the Bhar workers fail to do all works properly in time then to use abusive languages, have all bound some of the Bhar agricultural workers to react against Brahmans and plan not to render services to them. Tension then emerges from here between the two castes (Brahmans and Bhars) of villages Panjupur (Newada) and Ashrafpatti (Newada) respectively which ultimately takes the form of conflict at group level.

The inter-caste tension or conflict prevails in almost all the villages today. But intra-caste unity does not follow in equal amount. In comparison to other castes, the Brahman caste has a very weak informal organization. Because of the clash of interests within the caste and common interests with lower castes, the Brahmans show a weaker form of looser informal caste organization. The lower caste persons specially Bhars and Chamars choose their informal caste organization and unity within the caste as the utmost alternative for social security.

Casteism also seems to prevail in villages. All the castes studied have been reported to seek support of their respective caste leaders.

A competitive trend is apparent on village scene among different castes which have resulted in change in socio-economic and political spheres of lower castes and have started threatening the prestige of higher castes. The four castes, viz., Brahman, Kurmi, Bhar and Chamar have unfavourable attitude towards others which has created a dangerous situation to every caste studied. But Brahmans, in comparison to all other castes, feel a great social crisis and are afraid of lower castes (say, Bhar, and Kurmi). Bhar caste is emerging as a dominant caste because of its more numerical strength, economic freedom, good leadership, and local supports of other lower caste leaders. Bhars and Chamars are also afraid of higher castes but in less amount.

Non-cooperation movement on part of working lower castes have shaken the position of higher castes (Brahmans and Kurmis) who have now started seeking co-operation of other villages. The higher caste persons (Brahmans and Kurmis) being clever and because of being in power try to digest a major proportion of government facilities meant for lower poor castes. These all have given rise to inter-caste tension between higher and lower castes. As a result, every caste has its opponent castes and has begun to feel the possibility of open coercion. This is more apparent in Brahman caste than other castes. The higher caste persons have least high perception and hence most unfavourable attitude towards lower castes and likewise lower caste persons have least high perception and hence most unfavourable attitude towards higher castes. Both higher and lower caste persons discooperate each other and do not like to maintain village harmony. Lower caste persons (Bhar and Chamar) in a greater number do not like to work for higher caste persons of the respective villages and in lieu thereof the higher caste persons do not provide them the land facilities and other sorts thereof.

Before the changes which have taken place in socio-economic, political, and cultural aspects of Bhars and Chamars, they were accustomed to take the advice, guidance and support of Brahmans and Kurmis of their corresponding villages. They looked forward to the Brahmans and Kurmis for protection from external threats for arbitration in local disputes and also for personal affairs. But, today, Bhars and Chamars have been experiencing the law and judiciary as institutions for arbitrations in all sorts of disputes, affairs, and problems. Hence, we observe disconnection between advising and advised, service rendered and service rendering, protecting and protected castes. The old institutions have been replaced by new ones. The lower caste members are closely knitted than higher caste members as is evident from the fact that when conflict took place between Brahman (of Panjupur Newada) and Bhar (of Ashrafpatti, Newada), Bhars were more united than Brahmans. In Brahman caste, there were some opportunists who were not so sympathetic towards their own castemen. This refutes Coser's hypothesis that intergroup conflict leads to intra-group cohesiveness. The attendance of Bhar caste members found more in number than that of Brahman caste menbers. This indicates that consciousness among Bhar caste members is greater than that of Brahman caste members. A similar situation is also tangible in village Rabipur Bahauddinpur where Bhars are strongly united than Brahmans and Kurmis. The unity within the Bhar caste community and its non-cooperation movement against Brahman and Kurmi castes not to render their services to them by stopping their agricultural works of all sorts have made some of land-holding Brahmans and Kurmis to surrender before Bhars, so that Bhars may work and provide their agricultural services to them. In Brahman and Kurmi caste we thus observe the clash of interest within the caste. The members cut across their respective caste boundaries and show their alliance with Bhars resulting in division of village community in two factions. This finding is similar to the statement mentioned by Atal.[1] Atal writes, "Much social interaction in the Indian peasant community ... is not merely, nor even principally, inter-caste behaviour. This could be seen in the pattern of group alliances and faction formations. Membership in the faction cuts across kin and caste boundaries as a result either of a clash of interests within the caste or of a common interest between the people of different castes."

The Kurmis and Chamars of Hazipur Marui maintain their internal solidarity and their members cooperate their castemen. They, though, do not have ony formalized form of caste organization but as and when they feel some obstacles in their way, they call their castemen to discuss on specific matters. The observation revealed that the members attend any sort of informal meeting of their own caste and obey the decision taken in those meetings. This shows intra-caste cohesiveness within each caste group. Before conflict between Kurmi and Chamar, there was no unity upto the mark within each caste, but after conflict between the two,

1. Yogesh Atal, op. cit., 1968, p. 168.

over number of issues, intra-caste cohesiveness and solidarity within each caste is found tangible. This supports Coser's hypothesis that inter-group conflict leads to intra-group cohesiveness.

Dichotomy of conflict is more apparent in village Hazipur Marui than in other villages. The conflict between Kurmi and Chamar is dichotomic in the sense that the castes other than conflicting castes tend to support the dominant caste. In village Hazipur Marui, the weaker castes such as Lohar, Barhai, Loniya, and Dhobi are with Kurmi caste—a dominant group. This confirms Simmel's proposition that "conflict may also bring persons and groups together which have otherwise nothing to do with each other."[1]

Resolution of caste conflict is more or less tangible in village Hazipur Marui while in other villages under study, the conflict between different castes remains alive. The conflict in this village is resolved through institutional arrangement (court). For example, when Chamars of Hazipur Marui village lodged a writ in the court of Faizabad over an issue of a piece of land which the other castes including Kurmi were trying to capture, the final decision of the court went in the favour of Chamar. Since then, the overt conflict between the conflicting castes has gone to extinction but it does not mean that the latent conflict between them has also disappeared. It is not so, but it exists convertly and sometimes, appears manifest particularly at the time of village franchise for the village presidentship.

When two castes are in conflict, and if one caste is higher and predominant and the other is lower and predominated, the latter adopts certain customs and values and neglects other customs and values, of the former. While former does not do so as is evident in villages Panjupur (Newada) and Ashraf Patti (Newada) where Bhars adopt certain customs and values of Brahmans for the effective survival of the group and neglect the other customs and values of the Brahmans while Brahmans

1. George Simmel, *Conflict*, (trans.) Kurt H. Wolff, The Free Press, Glencoe, Illinois, 1955, p. 98.

can be termed as contributory reference group for Bhars but not vis-a-vis.

When two castes are in conflict and if one caste is predominant over the other and if the other caste succeeds in attaining its goal through institutional arrangement, the predominant caste becomes calm and quiet and begins to interact with the weaker caste. Now, the predominant caste tries to show its closeness with the opposite caste. Further, the weaker caste then begins to interpret this closeness according to their own ways and plead their social image and status similar to that of former. This is tangible in Hazipur Marui village where Chamars think so. They have, in this way, been able to enhance their social position in the village. Today Kurmis do not look at Chamars with the same angle with which they were looking at them before conflict. This infers that inter-caste conflict leads to change in attitude of conflicting castes towards each other. Now, Chamars of this village do not have in their hearts the same room for the Kurmis as they had for latter in past before conflict. Similar situation is also visible in case of Brahmans of Panjupur (Newada) where Bhars do not have the same respect for Brahmans as they had before conflict. This is also true in case of Rabipur Bahauddinpur.

In a conflict-situation between predominant higher and backward caste, a third caste, which also belongs to backward caste category and which is also aggrieved by the backward caste opposite to higher caste, due to the election of village presidentship, comes as intermediary and tries to organize the higher caste to strongly oppose the backward opponent in order to hit its two objectives: (i) to harass, boycott and discooperate the backward opponent; and (ii) to take revenge from higher caste as the latter had oppressed and depressed and ruled over the ancestors of intermediate caste group. Here, intermediate caste group as a side here plays a wicked role on the stage of rural drama to leave the hero marginal. These facts exist at the bottom of sea of inter-caste relationship of Rabipur Bahauddinpur village.

Conflict and Social Interaction between Castes

There is negative correlation between social interaction and conflict. The two are inversely related to each other. Social interaction between the conflicting castes tends to decrease with the increase in the intensity of conflict. Greater the intensity of inter-caste conflict, lesser will be the frequency of social interaction and contact between the conflicting castes.

The frequency of social and political interaction between the conflicting castes is also inversely connected to the intensity of conflict. In situation of acute conflict between opponent castes, the cleavages and line of demarcation become impossible to be embridged in social and political spheres. Not only this, but even social and political interaction between the conflicting castes becomes rare and possibly it may cease to continue.

In acute form of conflict between conflicting castes, even face to face interaction becomes least frequented. In such a situation, communication between opposing castes may also alter or may possibly disappear. Each caste begins to develop a negative image towards other.

No modernized techniques are used in conflict situation between rural castes. Verbal hot talks, abuses, scuffles, and attack by 'lathis' and bricks are the main techniques used in villages by different caste groups.

Complete interaction among different castes as a whole does not continue in villages, but latent tension among them always prevails.

Data tabulated on four variables viz., caste, age, education, and family type, have given a clearcut picture of the nature of respondents directly responsible for carrying out a tension-pocket for opponent castes in villages today. The 'Caste' has been taken as a main variable while other variables have been used differently on different responses.

Different hypotheses in the form of questions were put to test and the following conclusions have been drawn. In field situation it is found that these are nominally educated higher caste persons living in nuclear family and belonging to age group 25-35 who have unfavourable attitude towards lower caste persons (Bhar and Chamar). Similarly our findings related to lower caste respondents reveal that these are illiterate lower caste respondents living in nuclear family and belonging to age group 35-45 are directly responsible for the emergence, existence, and operation of tension and conflict between higher and lower castes. Such higher and lower caste respondents see each other suspiciously and feel negatively.

Appendix

Panjupur (Newada) and Ashraf Patti (Newada)

Punjupur (Newada)—a hamlet of village Panjupur—characterized by Brahman dominance in social, economic, political and cultural spheres have met conflicting situation with Ashraf Patti (Newada)—a village geographically unmarked and situated by the side of the former with the dominance of Bhar caste. The two dominant castes in their respective villages have shown a recorded sign of conflict in modern era. These villages though distinct from each other in official records of government, can be observed as a single unit by a foreigner to this area. For the purpose of present research work, however, both have been considered separately.

The Brahmans of Panjupur (Newada) have been accustomed to enjoy prestigious social position since antiquity. They used to employ Bhars of Ashrafpatti (Newada) as their agricultural workers. They gave only one Kilogram of superficial type of grain (sava or any other grain of this kind) to the Bhar workers. They always tried to take hard work from these workers and in case the workers failed to work hard, they used unparliamentary languages also. They considered themselves as lords and Bhar workers or Bhar caste as a whole as their slaves. These acts were practiced in greater amount by the older generation of Brahman caste and older generation of Bhar caste tolerated the same. Brahmans imposed their superiority upon the Bhars. But the time is not always static. It is dynamic in nature. With the dynamics of time, the conditions of social life get new shapes. New conditions are the consequences of changes occurred in social,economic, political and cultural spheres. Newly born conditions germinate new and absolutely new ideas in new generations. The past experiences stocked by olders are conveyed to the youngers. The youngers with new ideas and old experiences conveyed them through their ascendants develop a negative sense in themselves which lead to negative temperaments in them towards those who have ill-treated their ancestors.

In the year 1981, a Bhar named Hubraj was cutting grass in the field of a Brahman named Parmatma Shukla. There were crops in the field. Due to grass-cutting, some crops were destroyed. The grass-cutter was prohibited, some abuses and hot words were also used for him by Brahman. Next day, Lautu, the son of grass-cutter went to Parmatma and said, "why do you use hot words for my father." On this, some words were exchanged between the two. Hearing an unclear voice, some members of Bhar and Brahman castes gathered there. After this, they all went to their own houses. But, Bhars were using abuses for Brahmans from their houses in their own village.

The house of Parmatma Shukla is situated on the west side of his village Panjupur (Newada). There is a path which goes from eastern stream of village Panjupur (Newada) to south via nearby houses of Bhars. From that route, Udai Raj Shukla—a Brahman was going to his field to fetch food (maize) for his animals. Three members of Bhar caste named Bali Ram, Shri Ram and Mani Ram, who were sitting near the house of Jag Mohan—a Bhar, jointly attacked upon Udai Raj Shukla. He was charged lathis and bricks and ultimately earthed. Hearing some ambiguous news and voices, some Brahmans rushed towards the place and saw three Bhars beating Udai Raj Shukla. He had fallen on ground and was unconscious. About 6 or 7 persons belonging to Brahman caste tried to bring him home but at the same moment, 13 more Bhars gathered there and attacked by lathis and bricks on those who were trying to bring the severely tortured body. Some Brahmans were wounded but any way the body was brought home. At the same moment, Udai Raj Shukla breathed his last and lost his existence.

The suit was filed in Faizabad lower court. The decisions taken by two judges are enclosed herewith.

Researcher undertaking case study of a Bhar respondent of village Ashrafpatti (Newada).

The history known to the respondent starts from 1955. The Brahmans since antiquity have been accustomed to pay only one Kilogram of superficial type of grains and approximately half kilogram of crude cane sugar (Gur) for syrup. If the Bhars tried to go in other neighbouring villages to earn more, the Brahmans of Panjupur (Newada) used to oppress Bhars at all points, at all stages and used abusive languages including beating also. In case a Bhar tried to go to other villages, the Brahmans thinking that 'Then who shall plough'?, used to burn their dry-ripe-crops (Khalihan) and cut the green crops.

The Brahmans have always plotted against Bhars so that the latter should always be the slaves of the former. Bhars had been dependent upon Brahmans to enjoy irrigational facilities. Once, before 20 years they thought be independent and got their traditional facility—'Rahat' established but the

Brahmans got that stolen at a night so that Bhars might remain slaves and dependent. So far, Bhars were not hopeless. They made a plan to get a tube-well of their own and got success also. Some of their members began to watch their tube-well at night. This side, the Brahmans with the help of Police got them arrested with the charge that they had been moving at night illegally with illegal iron weapon (Bhala). The Police beat them severely and got one of them named 'Bipat' under their own custody and sent in jail at Faizabad who was left on bail after five days. The case was started. The Brahmans on one side used to beat approximately ten Bhars and on other side, they consoled fifteen of them in order to have them under their control.

Panchu Bhar was the worker of Late Pandit Udai Raj. He left the work because of old age. Udai Raj told him to send his son to work. The son named Minnu refused to work on one Kilogram (Ser at that time) of grain as he was getting at the rate of seven rupees per day at Akbarpur urban centre. One day when Minnu was returning his home in evening, five persons of Brahman caste attacked upon him in the way near the village garden. The case was, anyhow, lodged by Bhar in the Police Station concerned but the consequence was zero as the Sub-Inspector was in Brahman's favour on bribe-base. He drove away the lodgers—Bhars saying "Jao Sale, Vahan Kam Nahin Karte Ho, Baval Le Ke Aye Ho, Bhago Sale, Nahin To Haddi Tor Denge."

Such similar cases of the same nature of issue have frequently occurred in the villages and Bhars have always been the victim of Brahmans. In case, a Bhar fails to comply, he is abused, beaten and created hindrances on all walks by Brahmans.

One incidence is related to two Bhars who were going to attend the meeting of a Communist leader named Babar. In the way near the village, a Brahman named Sachcha Ram met and commented, "If you go to attend the meeting, note that we shall kill you both as we have taken subscription of fifty rupees from each Brahman household, and shall cast you in river Saryu." On this, a Bhar spoke, "Alright. We have 40-50 householders of own caste. We shall collect subscription from caste and kins and shall see you then." Next day nearly 22 or 23 Brahmans rushed towards that Bhar when he was operating his 'Rahat'—a traditional water-dropping-out instrument from well and started beating.

One day, Shri Ram—a Bhar by caste was cutting grass on a Chak-road near the field of a Brahman named Satya Narayan. Satya Narayan, seeing this grass cutter, rushed toward and abused and ordered to run away from there. On this Shri Ram claimed the same as public place and raised his voice not to go from there. Then Satya Narayan with the help of some other Brahmans wanted to beat Shri Ram but he ran away to escape his life.

In 1980-81, another Bhar named Bharathi was the worker of Pandit Udai Raj. One day, it was a hot season and the day was too hot to tolerate. Bharathi who was ploughing the field came earlier with the plea that the heat was intolerable. He wanted to drink cold water but Udai Raj ordered him to do other works first, then, to drink cold water. But Bharathi refused other works without drinking water and taking refreshment. On this, Panditji twisted his hand. Bharathi also tried to twist Brahman's hand, but, in the mid, some of the Brahman family members came at the place and beat this Bhar by hands and legs.

There is a garden in the village where a few boys of Bhar caste were playing on sticks a day. At seven or eight o'clock evening a Brahman, who was under the impression of alcoholism, while passing through the garden-way, listened to the stick's voice and noise. He stopped these and asked who they were and what they were doing. After knowing all the things in detail, he challenged that he would purchase all the Bhars and would uproot all of their households. During the same period another Brahman named Lallan Shukla came there and controlled the situation. But, next day morning, some Brahmans belonging to Panjupur (Newada) village reached the houses of some Bhars and in a organized way, they spoiled some of the small lemon trees and crushed some vegetable plants. When some other Bhars opposed such acts the Brahmans replied, "Be silent. We shall feed you what you will like to eat. Unless and until you are beaten, you shall not think of and care for our works." On this, Bhars responded, "You people are biased. You shall do whatever you shall like. We shall then raise our hands for your mercy if you attack upon us as we are poor persons before you. Two days before this matter, a Bhar known as Hub Raj had cut grass from the field of Parmatma—a Brahman fellow. Parmatma beat the Bhar and snatched his basket and grass cutting iron weapon—'Khurpa'. Next day, when the son of Hub Raj went to Parmatma and questioned, "Have you any specific mark of identification of your field's grass? You snatched the 'Khurpa'. You have also not paid my rickshaw charge which is due on you since two years back." After this Parmatma beat him twice by his stick. As this poor Bhar reached his home, about 20 or so Brahmans surrounded his house. The physical coercion took place between the Brahman and Bhar caste persons.

Rabipur Bahauddinpur which is the main hamlet of village Rabipur Bahauddinpur has been observed as the field of caste-conflict by the researcher. In this hamlet, there are three castes named Brahman, Kurmi and Bhar which are suspicious of each other. There is complex type of conflict in this village and it is not so easy for commoners to understand this kind of conflict. Even a social scientist without sharp perception and understanding can face difficulty in knowing the kind of conflict which has been undertaken by me to understand from sociological angle of vision. There is no complete involvement of members of each caste in the conflict. For example, not all Brahmins are completely involved in conflict with Bhars and Kurmis. Likewise, not all Kurmis are involved in conflict with Bhars and Brahmans. Similarly, not all Bhars oppose or show negative relations with all Brahmans and all Kurmis. To understand the physical and social structure of such conflict, a diagram has been found to be useful which can be seen as under:

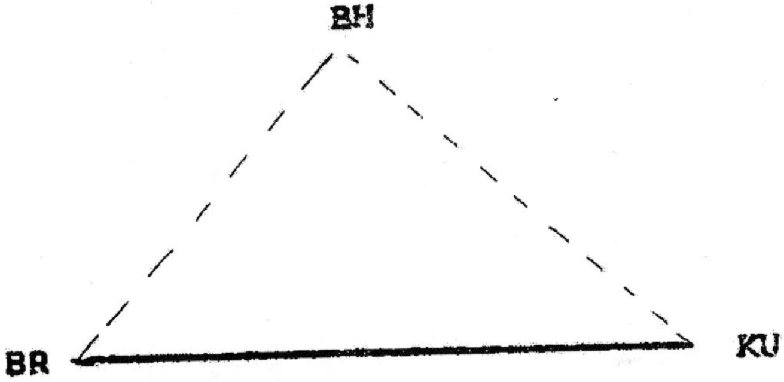

Diagram No. 1

In diagram 1, BR stands for Brahman
KU stands for Kurmi; and
BH stands for Bhar.
The straight line shows positive social relation or alliance while dotted line shows negative social relation.

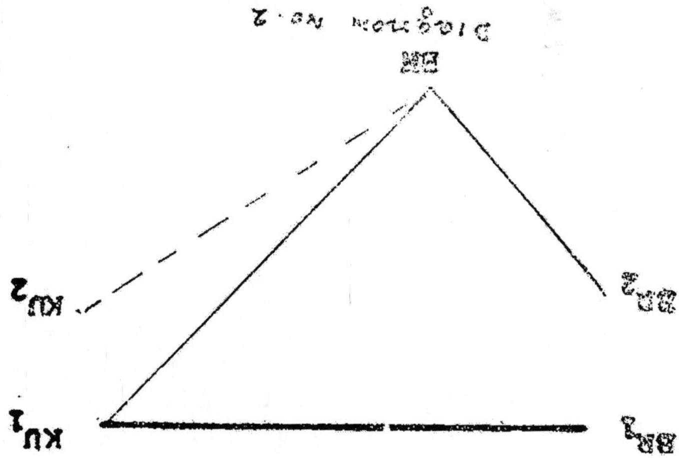

Diagram No. 2

In diagram No. 2 BR_1 stands for those Brahmans who have less land holding. Some of them have pride of their social prestige. BR_2 stands for those Brahmans who hold more lands and therefore they seek cooperation of Bhars for their agricultural work. KU_1 stands for those Kurmis who constitute majority of Kurmi caste population and they possess more land and like BR_2 they also want to seek cooperation of Bhars for agricultural purposes KU_2 stands for those Kurmis who are demographically less in number and some of them try to maintain their prestigious position in the hamlet and hence do not like to surrender before Bhars. BH stands for Bhars who have highest numerical strength in the hamlet.

As mentioned earlier in introductory note of this thesis that reveals that social life is always characterized as an admixure of co-operation and conflict. If at one point of time, there is peace and co-operation in a given system, it does not mean that they shall remain maintained in all the coming times. As the time fleets, conditions of the system get new shapes because of the changing as well as increasing needs of human race. If political needs are such social values which are looked as the measure and index of social status and hence social prestige, the different sections of the society try to win the same so that they can enhance their social position in the setting at micro as well as at macro level. The steps that each section of the society may take for attaining such values that section be caste or class, race or communal group, originates the faction thereby creating different factional groups where a sudden disturbance in the system is observed manifest.

Before the election of gram-pradhan in 1982, there was no factionalism in the hamlet and all the castes were enjoying a harmonious social life. In such a social situation there was more harmony and strength between Kurmi and Bhar castes. For example, the leader of Kurmi caste Shri Hari Ram Verma and the leader of Bhar caste Shri Gaya Prasad were the friends. They had warmth relation with each. To walk together, to sit together, to talk together, to discuss together on several social issues were their daily routines.

During the election there were seven contestants in the field for village presidentship. They were busy in propagating and convincing the people to vote for them. The population of the hamlet is nearly 1500 out of which there are 1000 listed voters in which Bhar caste has maximum number of voters. Gaya Prasad who was one of the contestants belonged to Bhar caste. He convinced his castemen to vote for him on the basis of caste. He ultimately used casteism as an instrument of victory and was finally elected. Previously, Hari Ram Verma M.L.A. Lok Dal and Gaya Prasad were fast friends but after election their friendship broke into pieces and they became segregated. Since then, all the Kurmi caste members tend to show negative attitude towards Bhars.

After the village election, there arose an occasion to elect members for village Panchayat. The contestants used the slogan of casteism for their victory. The feeling of casteism occupied a rigid or static place in the minds of the people and members were elected on the basis of caste.

After the election of village council, one day it so happened that a pet dog of Shyam Sundar Pandey was beaten by a person in tola or purwa of Bhars which is situated towards west of the hamlet. After being beaten, the dog came at its master's door in evening. This door is closed to the tola or Purwa of Bhars at the distance of one bigha. After hearing the dog's cry, Babu Lal Pandey the eldest son of Shyam Sundar Pandey said as to who had beaten the dog. After getting no response from the side of Bhars, he used few abusive words for them. At that time, Bhars did not speak even a single word nor did they give any response. But next day its consequences came into existence. On that day Bhar workers had to go to plant rice in the fields of Shyam Sundar Pandey, but they did not turn up to do so. The newly elected village president Gaya Prasad and Chinta Ram Bhar the leader of his own caste prohibited the Bhar workers not to go to render services to Shyam

Sundar Pandey. When this Brahman called upon the workers they answered not to go to him. They said, "You have unnecessarily abused us. We boycott you." A Bhar named Bahal who used to make the Brahman's buffalo graze grass also did not turn up on his usual duty that day morning. The field of the Brahman which was purposively prepared for the plantation of rice was full of water. The water was made available for the field since last night only so that in morning the field may be planted. In case the workers refused to come to do so, anyway the field was planted by the help of others not belonging to Bhar caste.

Day after that day, Ram Pratap who is Kurmi by caste went to Hari Ram Verma (a Kurmi) who although belongs to this hamlet but lives at Akbarpur town in the house of a Kurmi named Man Raj, and narrated the detailed story of such happening. Hearing the overall story, Hari Ram came to the hamlet and held a meeting in which the people belonging to Brahman and Kurmi castes assembled. In this meeting, it was decided to call Bhars. Bhars were informed to attend the meeting but they did not attend the meeting. This meeting was held in the headship of Hari Ram Verma who said that it was not an assault of an individual but an assault of Brahmans and Kurmis as a whole. He also said, "If today one Brahman has been boycotted by Bhars, tomorrow another Brahman shall be boycotted and next tomorrow a third one shall be boycotted. In this way all the non-Bhars shall be boycotted by Bhars. Therefore, it is necessary to make a strong front against Bhar organization in order to face them so that they may not commit such mistake in future against us." As a consequence, a caste alliance or amalgamation of two dissimilar or unanalogous castes viz., Brahman and Kurmi was formed in the hamlet against Bhars. This caste alliance aimed at looking down the Bhars. This aim was supported by all the members of Brahman and Kurmi castes.

Previously, all the members may be of Brahman or Kurmi caste did not believe each other. They saw each other suspiciously. When the question of organizational set up to fight against Bhars arose, the members of Brahman and Kurmi castes were told to take an oath taking a glass of Ganges water to remain organized and maintain the unity among themselves for their social survival. This ritual was performed to confirm harmony, unity, faith, friendship, solidarity and strength among them. They said, "we shall accompany each other and shall not show trickery against any body in the organization. These statements can be seen diagrammatically through diagram No. 1 shown in beginning of this section.

It is true that the formation of an organization is interest based but it is also true that the feelings and emotions also function in the formation of an organization. The feelings and emotions of an individual or individuals of a group are not static but they are proportional to time and space. As the time varies, feelings and emotions of an individual or individuals also vary. For example, a high tension individual or aggressive personality is not always aggressive, but he may be low tension individual peaceful in other social situation at another point of time. Similarly, a low tension individual or peaceful personality is not always peace ful in all social situations at all points of time but he may be highly tensive or aggressive in a situation where he is assaulted or his interests are killed by others.

When an individual finds his interests unfulfilled or dissatisfied in an organization, he conciders such organization as useless or futile for him. Here, he tends to withdraw his membership from such organization and plans another strategy to satisfy his needs. Some of the Brahmans and Kurmis who had more landholding as compared to others in their own caste community found it very costly and trouble some to employ agricultural workers of other villages or of the villages of their kinsmen. They then thought it better to adapt with Bhars and develop positive relationship with them by interacting and showing sympathy and co-operation with Bhars so that Bhar workers of the hamlet be agree to work in their fields. Here, we find fusion in Brahman as well as in Kurmi castes and their fission with Bhar caste. The base of such fussion and fision is oniy the selfishmese of such Brahmans and Kurmis who want to satisy their agricultural needs by such behaviour. This behaviour of selfish Brahmans and Kurmis deeply shocked the original organizational front of the Brahman and Kurmi castes. Not only this but those who were amalgamated with Bhar caste even tried to pretend others to go with them. Few persons belonging to Brahman and Kurmi caste even went to join the company of Bhar caste. Since then, the whole hamlet is totally disturbed and surrounded by conflict. The form of such conflict in which different components are involved may those components be in the form of caste or caste-split has been shown in diagram No. 2 mentioned earlier.

One day, two members belonging to Bhar caste named Afat and Bhikha were bringing a pair of bullocks through the field of a Kurmi named Ram Kewal Verma. When Ram Kewal Verma refrained (checked) them not to go through his field, they avoided and did not pay attention and they forcibly tried to pass through field with bullocks. On this, some hot words were exchanged among them and both the parties were committed to beat eath other. Ultimately, Afat attacked upon Ram Kewal and beat him once by a bomboo and wounded his head. Thereafter, Ram Kewal and his associates lodged F.I.R. against them. Sub-Inspector (Police) took approximately 10-12 persons belonging to Bhar caste under his custody and kept them at Police Station Akbarpur for a night and beat them severely. Next day, they were left on bail. Litigation concerning this matter is going on.

The conflict between Kurmi and Bhar castes has affected the social structure of hamlet on one hand and directly affected the Bhar caste on the other hand. For example, when at one night theft took pleace in the house of a Bhar, he cried out the people to help him. The people of the hamlet awoke but none came at his house to help. Some persons went there while thieves had been successful in running away with stolen property. Here, we observe social change in the hamlet. For instance, when there was no factionalism in the hamlet, all the people rushed towards the place where happenings of such or any other sort took place and there was unity and co-operation among all castes and thus in hamlet as a whole, but after the factional polities casteism and caste disputes, the unity of the hemlet people was deeply hampered.

Researcher discussing on several issues of inter caste tension and undertaking a case study of a leader of Chamar caste in village Hazipur Marui.

There was a dispute among different castes over a piece of land. In 1968, a Panchayat was held in the village in which the matter was not finalized. Dispute continued which tended to take a form of caste-riot but it could not happen so. As a consequence, the village people were divided into two factions. One faction consisted of all Chamars while other faction consisted of all other castes named Kurmi, Barhai, Lohar, Loniya and Dhobi. A writ was lodged in court concerning the matter in which decision went in favour of Chamars. Other castes felt a great discomfiture (defeat). A Conciliation was proposed to join all the castes and the land came in possession of Chamars.

In 1972, an election of village Panchayat was held in which signs of tension were observed between the two parties which still goes on continued. As a result of village franchise, Ram Lutavan Verma, a Kurmi, was elected as village President.

There is another piece of land lying in between two

Harijan (untouchables) dwellings which is also the main path of Harijans as well as of whole villagers. The village President Mr. Lutavan Verma proposed to construct building of Co-operative Society but Chamars of the village opposed not to get building constructed and they faced the dispute and were successful which gave rise to continuity of tension.

Again in 1982, election of village Panchayat was proposed to be held. Mr. Ram Lutavan Verma ex-village president was one of the contestants. Besides this, both the parties had got their own contestants. They canvassed, supported and voted for their respective candidates but ultimately Mr. Ram Lutavan Verma was elected. The continuity of conflict between the two factional groups still remains observable.

Bibliography

Atal, Yogesh, The Changing Frontiers of Caste, National Publishing House, Delhi, 1968.

Bailey, F.G., Caste and the Economic Frontier, Manchester University Press, 1957.

Brass, Paul, R., Factional Politics in an Indian State: The Congress Party in Uttar Pradesh, University of California Press, Barkeley, 1965.

Brend, W., The Foundations of Human Conflict, London, 1944.

Cantril, H., *Tension that causes war*, Urbana, 1950.

Chitambar, J.B., Introductory Rural Sociology, John Wiley and Sons, New York, 1973.

Coser, Lewis, A., The Functions of Social Conflict, Routledge and Kegan Paul Ltd., London, 1956.

Dahrendorf, Ralf, Class and Class Conflict in Industrial Society, Routledge and Kegan Paul, Ltd., London, 1959.

Davis, K., Human Society, Macmillan Co., New York, 1969.

Dubey, S.C., Indian Village, Routledge and Kegan Paul Ltd., London, 1955.

Durant, Will, The Story of Civilisation (Part I—our Oriental Heritage), Simon and Schuster, New York, 1954.

Durkheim, Emile, *Suicide: A study in Sociology*, Kegan Paul Ltd., London, 1966.

Edward, L.P., The Natural History of Revolution, Chicago, 1927.

Ghurye, G.S., Caste and Class in India, Popular Book Depot, Bombay, 1957.

Ghurye, G.S., Social Tensions in India, Popular Prakashan, Bombay, 1968.

Goode, W.J. and Hatt, P.K., Methods in Social Research, McGraw Hill, Kogakusha Ltd., 1952.

Guha, B.S., Studies in Social Tensions Among the Refugees from Eastern Pakistan, Government of India Press, Calcutta, 1959.

Gupta, Giri Raj, Cohesion and Conflict in Modern India, Vikas Publishing House, New Delhi, 1978.

Heimsath, Charles, H., Indian Nationalism and Hindu Social Reform, Princeton University Press, Bombay, Oxford University Press, 1964.

Henry, Cronstein, Gaon: Conflict and Cohesion in Indian Village, Princeton University Press, New Jersey, 1665.

Haughes, E.C., Conflict and the Web of Group Affliations, Glencoe, 1955.

Hunashal, S.M., The Lingayat Movement, Karnatak Sahitya Mandir, Dharwar, 1947.

Huttan, J.H., Caste in India, Oxford University Press, Bombay, 1961.

Kretch, D. and Crutchfield, R.S., Theory and Problems of Social Psychology, Mc-Graw Hill, New York, 1948.

Lewin, Kurt, Resolving Social Conflict, Harper Brothers Publishers, New York, 1948.

Lewis, Oscar, Group Dynamics in a North Indian Village, A Study of Factions, Delhi, 1954.

Martindale, Don, Social Life and Cultural Change, D. Van Nostrand Co., Princeton, 1962.

Mukherjee, R.K., Inter-Caste Tensions: Caste Tension Studies, Lucknow University, Lucknow, 1951.

Murphy, Gardner, In the Minds of Men, Basic Books, New York, 1953.

Nehru, Jawahar Lal, The Discovery of India, Meridian Books Ltd., London, 1956.

Paranjape, A.C., Caste Prejudice and the Individual, Bombay, Lalvani Publishing House, 1970.

Parsons, Talcott, The Social System, The Free Press, Glenooe, Illinois, 1951.

Prasad, N., Jati Vyavastha, Raj Kamal Prakashan, Delhi, 1965.

Prasad, R.N., Caste-Prejudice among College Students, Rupa Psychological Centre, Bhelupura, Varanasi, 1979.

Radhakrishnan, S., The Hindu View of Life, George Allen and Unwin Ltd., London, 1954.

Ramchandra Raj, G., Functions and Dysfunctions of Social Conflict, Popular Prakashan, Bombay, 1974.

Rastogi, P.N., The Nature and Dynamics of Factional Conflict, The Macmillan Company of India Limited, Delhi, 1975.

Simmuel, George, Conflict, The Free Press, Glencoe, Illinois, 1955.

Singh, K.K., Patterns of Caste Tension, Asia Publishing House Bombay, 1967.

Sinha, Surjit, Caste in India: A Trend Report in a Survey of Research in Sociology and Social Anthropology, Popular Prakashan, Bombay, 1974.

Sorokin, P.A., The Crisis of Our Age, New York, 1957.

Sorokin, P.A., Sociological Theories of Today, Harper and Row, New York, 1966.

Srinivas, M.N , India's Villages, Asia Publishing House, Bombay, 1960.

Srinivas, M.N., Caste in Modern India and other Essays, Bombay: Asia, 1962.

The Nature of Conflict (UNESCO), 1957.

Vakil, C.N. and Cabinetmaker, P.N., Government and Displaced Persons: A study in Social Tensions, Bombay, 1956.

Weber, Max, The Methodology of Social Science, The Free Press, Glencoe, Illinois, 1949.

Weber, Max, The Protestant Ethic and Spirit of Capitalism, Unwin University Books, London, 1968.

Young, P.V., Scientific Social Survey and Research, Prentice Hall of India Pvt. Ltd., New Delhi, 1975.

Zinkin, T., Caste Today, Bombay: Oxford University Press, 1962.

Journals

Alexander, F., "Discussion on Hostility and Fear in Social Life", Social Forces, Vol. 17, 1948.

Anant, S.S., "Caste Hindu Attitudes towards Harijans", Journal of Social Psychology, 1970.

Barth, Frederic, "Segmentary Opposition and the Theory of Games", Journal of the Royal Anthro-political Institute, 1959.

Bougle, C., "The Essence and Reality of the Caste System", Contribution to Indian Sociology, Vol. II (Ed. Dumont and Pocock), 1958.

Dahrendorf, Ralf, Towards a Theory of Social Conflict", The Journal of Conflict Resolution, 1958.

Dixit, R.C. and Sharma, D.D., "Transformation of Social Values of different Castes", Psychologia: An International Journal of Psychology in the Orient, 1970.

Ishwaren, K., "Caste and Social Tension in South India", Social Integration in India, I.S.S. Agra University, Agra, 1961.

Joshi, P., "Caste as it exists today", Indian Psychology, 1968.

Kane, J.J., Protestant-Catholic Tensions", Sociological Review, 1951.

Rastogi, P.N., "Faction Situation at Brahminpura", Man in India, 1963.

Rath, R. and Sircar, N.C., "Inter-Caste relationship as reflected in the study of attitudes and opinions of six Hindu caste Groups", Journal of Social Psychology, 1960.

Singh, U.P. and Bhusan, L.I., "Caste-Stereotypes: An Inter-perceptual Analysis", Proceedings of the 50th Session of Indian Science Congress Association, Bombay, 1969.

Institutional Publications

Encyclopaedia Britannica, No. 14.

(a) Census Report, 1961.

(b) Census Report, 1971, Series 21, Part XA, and Part XB.

(c) Census Manuscript 1961, obtained from office of the Tahsildar, Akbarpur (Faizabad).

District Gazetteers of the United Provinces, Vol. XLIII, Faizabad, 1928.

International Encyclopaedia of Social Sciences, No. 3 and 4.

Report of Executive Engineer (Canal) Faizabad for the year 1977-78 regarding irrigational facilities available for the rural people of Faizabad district.

Report of Bhu Lekha Adhikari, Faizabad for the year 1977-78.

(1) Report of Block Development Officer, Faizabad on irrigational facilities, 1977-78.

(2) Report of District Agricultural Officer, Faizabad, 1977-78.

Sankhyikiya Patrika, District Faizabad, 1978.

Uttar Pradesh District Gazetteers, Faizabad, 1960.

Index